MW00712898

10

GUIDELINES TO GREATNESS

DAVID COOPER

10

Unless otherwise indicated, Scripture quotations are taken from *The Holy Bible, New International Version*®. NIV®. Copyright © 1973, 1978, 1984, 2011 by International Bible Society. Used by permission of Zondervan Publishing House. All rights reserved.

Scripture quotations marked CJB are taken from *Complete Jewish Bible*®. Copyright © 1998 by David H. Stern. Used by permission. All rights reserved.

Scripture quotations marked CSB are taken from *The Christian Standard Bible*®. Copyright © 2017 by Holman Bible Publishers. Christian Standard Bible®, and CSB® are federally registered trademarks of Holman Bible Publishers. Used by permission. All rights reserved.

Scripture quotations marked ESV are taken from *The Holy Bible, English Standard Version*. Copyright © 2005 by Crossway Bibles, a division of Good News Publishers. Used by permission. All rights reserved.

Scripture quotations marked *KJV* are taken from the King James Version of the Bible.

Scripture quotations marked *NKJV* are taken from the *New King James Version*. Copyright © 1979, 1980, 1982, 1990, 1995, Thomas Nelson, Inc., Publishers.

Director of Publications: David W. Ray
Managing Editor of Publications: Lance Colkmire
Editorial Assistant and Copy Editor: Tammy Hatfield
Graphic and Layout Design: Michael McDonald

ISBN: 978-1-64288-129-5

Copyright © 2021 by Pathway Press
1080 Montgomery Avenue
Cleveland, Tennessee 37311

All rights reserved. No part of this publication may be reproduced or transmitted in any form or by any means, electronic or mechanical, including photocopying, recording, or otherwise, or by any information storage or retrieval system, without the permission in writing from the publisher. Please direct inquiries to Pathway Press, 1080 Montgomery Avenue, Cleveland, TN 37311.

Visit *www.pathwaypress.org* for more information.

CONTENTS

INTRODUCTION

The English historian Macauley cautioned the American people years ago that our Constitution ran the risk of being "all sail and no anchor." Our moral foundation has changed from the solid rock of Biblical values to the shifting sands of moral relativism where every person does what is right in their own eyes.

God engraved the Ten Commandments in stone, not sand, for a reason. Stone is permanent while sand washes away with each changing of tides. God gave Ten commandments—not suggestions or considerations or viewpoints—for the most excellent way to live. The commandments are an expression of God's love that give us an ethical compass for happy and healthy living.

It's easy to dismiss the Ten Commandments as no longer applicable, since Jesus said He came to fulfill the Law. That's not what He meant. "Christ is the culmination of the Law so that there may be righteousness for everyone who believes" (Romans 10:4). The word *culmination* is also translated "end, goal, or fulfillment." The Law is needed to reveal our sin and lead us to Christ the Savior, but it can't save; only Jesus saves!

The Ten Commandments embody divine truth that cuts across generational lines. Truth transcends time.

"For everything that was written in the past was written to teach us, so that through the endurance taught in the Scriptures and the encouragement they provide we might have hope" (Romans 15:4).

Let's journey back in time and discover the power of the Ten Commandments that God has forever written on our hearts.

1
STONE, NOT SAND

"And God spoke all these words. . . ."

Exodus 20:1

Since we were on our family vacation, I did something I wouldn't ordinarily do—I watched a television talk show. The show was *Oprah Winfrey*, and the subject was *morality*.

Now, this ought to be interesting, I thought.

The program featured a panel of guests, a psychologist, and, of course, the audience.

The following scenario was presented: "If you had the power of life and death, and could speak death over a person and never get caught, would you, do it? Would you actually take someone's life?"

Three members of the audience were selected at random to answer the question. The first lady answered, "Yes." When Oprah asked who, she said, "I'd rather not say." (A touch of wisdom amidst the madness of it all.)

"Yes, I would do it without a second thought," responded a young man.

The third person, a young lady, said, "Yes, I would do it."

When Oprah asked who, she replied, "Someone at my church."

Stunned, Oprah turned to the psychologist and asked what he thought about their responses.

"I'm shocked by what I'm hearing," he said. "Their responses are frightening. These people would commit murder if they knew they wouldn't get caught. Their morals are determined by the fear of consequences rather than being directed by an inner moral code."

People are losing their inner moral code. It's like we are living in the period of the Old Testament judges, when "everyone did as they saw fit" (Judges 21:25). God engraved the Ten Commandments in stone for a reason—stone is permanent. Truth transcends time and remains constant in every generation.

One study showed only 14 percent of Americans could name all of the Ten Commandments. Seven of the Ten Commandments are familiar to less than half of Americans, including "Honor your mother and father" and "Remember the Sabbath."[1]

Historically, social order is based on a moral consensus of the people derived from religious truth. Historian Will Durant said, "No civilized society has ever been able to survive in history without a strong moral code. Nor has there ever been a moral code that was not formed by religion."

Over the years, a slow gradual erosion of our moral consensus based on Judeo-Christian ethics has taken place in our public institutions, religious centers, and personal morality, pushing us toward social disintegration.

---

[1] "Ten Commandments Study" (9/2007 Kelton Research), cited in *annroeker.com*.

The fact that America's democratic republic was founded on Judeo-Christian ethics embodied in the Ten Commandments and the teachings of Jesus is being discounted today.

Future Past

History speaks for itself. James Madison wrote: "We have staked the whole future of the American civilization, not upon the power of government, far from it. We have staked the future upon the capacity of each and all of us to govern ourselves, to control ourselves, to sustain ourselves, according to the Ten Commandments of God."

George Washington said, "It is impossible to rightly govern the world without God and the Bible."

John Adams stated, "The highest glory of the American Revolution was this: It connected in one indissoluble bond the principles of civil government with the principles of Christianity."

Joseph Story, in his 1829 inaugural address as Dane Professor of Law at Harvard University, stated: "There has never been a period in which common law did not recognize Christianity as laying at its foundation."

In a *Newsweek* article titled, "How the Bible Made America," the authors wrote that the Bible has for centuries "exerted an unrivaled influence on American culture, politics, and social life. Now historians are discovering that the Bible, perhaps even more than the Constitution, is our founding document: the source of the powerful myth of the United States as a special, sacred nation, a people called by God to establish a model society, a beacon to the world."

The article also reported, "There were times, too, when Bible study was the core of public education and nearly every literate family not only owned a Bible but read from it regularly and reverently." Because of this pervasive Biblical influence, the United States seemed to Europeans to be one vast congregation, as G. K. Chesterton said, "with the soul of a church."[2]

I am not trying to revise history by suggesting that at one time all Americans were deeply religious, or that the nation has always lived by the rule of God. We have not. The government's mistreatment of Native Americans, the institution of slavery, segregation, and abortion on demand stand among our great sins.

However, Abraham Lincoln correctly observed in his Gettysburg Address that America is "a nation conceived in liberty and dedicated to the proposition that all men are created equal." He appealed to our core values embodied in the Declaration of Independence and the Constitution that are derived from Scripture to end the Civil War, to eradicate slavery, and to establish "a more perfect union." The nation's foundation is one of faith and obedience to God's law to "love your neighbor as you love yourself." It is no accident that our currency declares, "In God We Trust." Our only hope is to return to our foundation of faith in God and to the moral truth found in the Bible.

While we retain the symbols of faith, we often forfeit the substance of our faith. We see the symbols of faith everywhere. Congress opens every session with prayer.

---

[2] Kenneth L. Woodward and David Gates, "How the Bible Made America," *Newsweek* (Dec. 27, 1982), 44-51.

The President is sworn into office with his hand on the Bible. The Supreme Court clerk opens sessions daily by announcing "God save this honorable court." The Liberty Bell bears an inscription from the Book of Leviticus: "Proclaim liberty throughout the land unto all the inhabitants thereof" (25:10 KJV).

We often say one thing and do another. For example, during a *New York Times* interview, a noted Christian businessman was asked what he believed in. He replied, "I believe in God, the family, and McDonald's hamburgers. And when I get to the office, I reverse the order." Perhaps he was only trying to be humorous, but he aptly described how many people live by a double standard. We see this double standard, between private life and public life, on a national scale.

The real question we must answer is the one posed by the psalmist: "If the foundations be destroyed, what can the righteous do?" (Psalm 11:3 KJV).

Slippery Slope

In C. S. Lewis' classic *The Screwtape Letters*, Screwtape tells Wormwood: "The safest road to Hell is the gradual one—the gentle slope, soft underfoot, without sudden turnings, without milestones, without signposts."[3] Whether we want to admit it or not, America stands on the slippery slope of spiritual decay.

The culture war is about the definition and the source of truth. Is truth objective or subjective? Is truth absolute or relative? Does truth come from God or from us? Do we value "my truth" over *the truth*? Are we supposed to

---

[2] C. S. Lewis, *The Screwtape Letters* (New York: Mentor Books, 1988), XI.

stop asking, "Is it right?" and only ask, "Does it work?" Pragmatism applies to engineering but not to ethics. Just because something works doesn't make it right. The end does not justify the means. The means must be ethical if the end is going to be beneficial. Just because we *can* do something doesn't mean we *should* do it.

People today often call good evil and evil good. God warns us, "Woe to those who call evil good and good evil, who put darkness for light and light for darkness, who put bitter for sweet and sweet for bitter" (Isaiah 5:20). Such an inversion of values is most obvious in the multi-billion-dollar-a-year-enterprise of abortion on demand. Many of the same people who claim to stand for social justice and civil and human rights, deny the right to life to the most innocent—the unborn child in the safety of their mother's womb. Late-term and partial-birth abortions (for non-medical emergencies) are not pro-choice; they are anti-life. Clearly, that's calling good evil and evil good.

What Is Truth?

When Pilate questioned Jesus, he asked Him, "What is truth?" That's the question of our times as well. Alan Bloom, in *The Closing of the American Mind*, says, "Almost every student entering the university believes or says that he believes that truth is relative." Moral relativism rules the day. Many people only do what is right in their own eyes with a disregard for what is right in God's eyes. The secular world advocates tolerance for everything except the truth.

When novelist Walker Percy was asked what concerned him most about America's future, he answered,

"Probably the fear of seeing America, with all its great strength and beauty and freedom . . . gradually subside into decay through default and be defeated, not by the Communist movement, demonstrably a bankrupt system, but from within, from weariness, boredom, cynicism, greed and, in the end, helplessness before its great problems."[4]

We need divine truth to give us light in the darkness, a shelter from the storm, and a foundation on which to stand. Truth is found only in the person of Jesus and the authority of Scripture. In the stage play *1776*, John Adams is portrayed pacing the floor during the session of the Continental Congress in Philadelphia. The debate was deadlocked determining our country's course to either return to colonialism or emerge as a free nation. His heart is filled with anguish. His soul struggles with these lonely questions: *Is anyone there? Does anyone see what I see? Does anyone care?*

Psychologists tell us what we need is more self-esteem and to realize we're not so bad after all. Immoral and unethical behavior are redefined in terms of low self-esteem and environmental conditions.

Politicians tell us we need to raise taxes and increase federal programs. Yet, while we spend more on social causes, poverty, crime, violence, and failing schools, the breakdown of the family continues to rise, especially in our urban centers.

Educators tell us moral problems stem from a lack of education. Knowledge is the key to reversing the trends of moral and social decay, according to some advocates.

---

[4] Charles Colson, *The Body* (Thomas Nelson, 1992), 9.

This idea dates to Aristotle, who believed education would eventually erase sin and evil. This idea gained great prominence during the Enlightenment, when philosophy shifted its focus from God to man. Jean Jacques Rousseau argued that people were basically good were it not for the evil, corrupting influences of societies and governments. He said, "Vices belong less to man than to man badly governed."[5] (Oh, I get it—it's the government's fault.) Social breakdown comes from poor ethics, not poor education. After all, "The fear of the Lord is the beginning of knowledge" (Proverbs 1:7). Education is incomplete without ethics.

Sociologists tell us we can build a utopia through social engineering, community programs, and global government. Karl Marx's influence plunged Eastern Europe into the dark ages by the errors of socialism and communism in the twentieth century. Our feeble efforts to cure our nation's ills through social programs and government intervention have made us more dependent on the government than ever, even though we pride ourselves on our independence.

Do we think we can build the city of man without the city of God? Will we not relive the Tower of Babel? *Babel* means "confusion," which is always the state of things when we leave God out of our plans. While we do need to share our wealth, combat poverty, provide quality education, and empower our youth, we cannot reach these goals without the virtues of individualism, independence, and initiative. Our culture is obsessed over rights while it neglects personal responsibility. Every person needs to

---

[5] Charles Colson, *The Body*, 176-177.

be responsible to work and to produce for their own success. While we help those who cannot help themselves, we must require responsible work for all who can work.

What God Says

Our greatest need is spiritual—not political, social, economic, or educational. Like ancient Israel in the desert, we need to assemble ourselves at the base of Mount Sinai and hear the Word of God as He speaks to us today:

And God spoke all these words:

I am the Lord your God, who brought you out of Egypt, out of the land of slavery.

You shall have no other gods before me.

You shall not make for yourself an idol in the form of anything.

You shall not misuse the name of the Lord your God.

Remember the Sabbath day by keeping it holy.

Honor your father and your mother.

You shall not murder.

You shall not commit adultery.

You shall not steal.

You shall not give false testimony against your neighbor.

You shall not covet.

We need to rediscover the Ten Commandments. We need to accept God's right to command our obedience. He has the right because He is our Creator and "we are his people, the sheep of his pasture" (Psalm 100:3). God gave us the Law because He loves us. His law leads to abundant life. When you listen to your conscience, you will hear God's law guiding you when making moral decisions. Long before Moses received the law on tablets of stone, God inscribed His law on people's hearts. People "show that the requirements of the law are written on their hearts, their consciences also bearing witness" (Romans 2:15).

The problem is we all have a sin nature. Sin silences the voice of the Law so that we are deaf to its commandments. Consequently, we grope around lost in the darkness of moral relativism. We think we know the difference between right and wrong, but we don't. "There is a way that seems right to man but its end is the way to death" (Proverbs 16:25 ESV).

Law and Grace

You may be thinking, *We're living in the day of grace. What does the Law have to do with us?* After all, the Bible says, "The law was given through Moses; grace and truth came through Jesus Christ" (John 1:17). Let's take a moment to reflect on why God gave us the Law.

When Israel came out of Egypt, after four hundred years of slavery, she emerged as a new nation. A nation so unique that Moses told them they were "[the Lord's] treasured possession . . . a kingdom of priests and a holy nation" (Exodus 19:5-6). All civilized societies are built on laws without which society degenerates into anarchy.

Three categories of laws were provided to govern the life of the new nation of Israel. First, God gave them the *moral law*, or the Ten Commandments—the basis of morality. God also gave them *civil laws* to govern relationships, the home, and society. Finally, God gave them *ceremonial laws*, concerning the priests, the sacrifices, the tabernacle, and the holy days, to govern their worship and to teach them the meaning of God's redeeming grace.

While the civil and ceremonial laws are filled with rich meaning, they are also time-bound and culturally sensitive. They relate specifically to the formation and perpetuation of Israel as a distinct nation. The moral law, however, was engraved in stone. It transcends time, culture, and ethnicity, providing every generation a guiding light amid moral darkness.

So, why do we need the Ten Commandments?

The Ten Commandments reveal sin. Without the commandments we have no knowledge or definition of sin. "Therefore no one will be declared righteous in God's sight by the works of the law; rather, through the law we become conscious of our sin" (Romans 3:20).

The Ten Commandments lead us to Christ. When we come face to face with our sinfulness, we recognize our need of a Savior. The Law was given to lead us to Christ (Galatians 3:4). When we come to God in confession (admitting our sin) and repentance (willing to change the way we're living), He forgives us and cleanses us from our sins (1 John 1:9). God delivers us from the power of sin so sin no longer controls us.

The Ten Commandments teach us how to live happy and healthy lives. "Walk in obedience to all that the Lord your God has commanded you, so that you may live and prosper and prolong your days in the land that you will possess" (Deuteronomy 5:33).

By Grace Through Faith

Contrary to popular opinion, people in Old Testament times were not saved from their sins by keeping the Law. The Bible says in no uncertain terms that "no [one] will be justified in His sight by [observing] the law" (Romans 3:20 NKJV). To be "justified" means to be pardoned from sin and to be declared righteous in God's sight. Salvation has always been by grace through faith. God was, is, and always will be the God of grace. The word *grace* means "gift."

When Adam and Eve sinned in the Garden of Eden, did God give them the Law for their salvation? Absolutely not! God provided them external coverings made from animal skins as a sign that He covered their sins by atonement. The sacrificial animal in Eden took their place. The animal died in their place. This was a type of Jesus' sacrifice on the Cross. He took our guilt so we might be pardoned. The coverings they received were provided by God's grace, not their works.

Noah and his family weren't saved from the Flood because he was better than everybody else. "Noah found grace in the eyes of the Lord" (Genesis 6:8 NKJV). God's grace was extended to everyone just as it was to Noah. Grace warned the people to repent and to save themselves from the coming flood. But they refused the grace of God to their own peril. Only Noah responded to God's grace with faith.

Abraham is the father of Israel and of all who put their faith in Jesus. He wasn't righteous because He kept the Law. In fact, he lived at least six hundred years before the Law was given. "Abraham believed [God], and it was credited to him as righteousness" (15:6). The example of Abraham's faith which justified him before God occupies center stage in the New Testament.

The so-called "faith chapter" of the Bible tells the story of all the Old Testament heroes who lived by faith. Twenty-four times the writer pens the words "by faith." He celebrates their legacy by writing, "These were all commended for their faith" (Hebrews 11:39).

So, salvation from sin has never been provided by keeping the Law. Eternal salvation and forgiveness of sin are always by God's grace received by faith alone. The people who lived before the coming of Jesus looked ahead in faith to Messiah's coming. We who live after His coming look back in faith to His death, resurrection, and ascension. Regardless of history, we all look to Jesus for salvation. They anticipated redemption while we live in the accomplishment of redemption. The perspectives are different, but the principle is the same—God's people live *by faith!*

Saul (who became the Apostle Paul) spent years trying to justify himself by keeping the Law. Then He met Jesus on the Damascus Road and learned only God can make a person righteous. He wrote, "For it is by grace you have been saved, through faith—and this not from yourselves, it is the gift of God—not by works, so that no one can boast" (Ephesians 2:8-9).

Balancing Act

Let's recap what we've learned about Law and grace: People have never been saved by keeping the Law. God did not give us rules to get us to Heaven. He gave us His Son to get us to Heaven. God gave us the Law to reveal our sin so we would turn to Jesus to save us. He also gave the Law as a moral compass for holy, happy, and healthy living.

A sign posted at the entrance to a convent where nuns lived read: "Trespassers will be prosecuted to the fullest extent of the law." It was signed by, "The Sisters of Mercy."

Grace and God's law go hand in hand. The God of grace spoke from Mount Sinai and gave the Law. The Law is an expression of God's love given for our benefit. A perfect balance exists between grace and Law. Law was born out of grace. If we go to one extreme or the other, the balance of truth is lost. If we overemphasize the Law, we become legalists boasting about how righteous we are. On the other hand, if we twist the meaning of grace, we turn the grace of God into a license for sin. But grace doesn't free us *to* sin; it frees us *from* sin.

Grace saves us from our sins and fulfills the righteousness of the Law in our lives. As a result, we have both the desire and ability to obey the Law. God says, "I will make a new covenant. . . . I will put my law in their minds and write it on their hearts" (Jeremiah 31:31, 33). The Apostle Paul wrote, "Therefore, there is now no condemnation for those who are in Christ Jesus, because through Christ Jesus the law of the Spirit of life has set you free from the law of sin and death . . . in order that the righteous requirement of the law might be fully met in us" (Romans 8:1-4).

Think of it—everything the Law requires has been fully met because of what Jesus has done for us! The righteousness of the Law is given to us through our faith in Jesus, who is our righteousness!

God's GPS

The Ten Commandments is God's GPS for life. When our family travels, Barbie invariably cautions me to stay on the prescribed route. She knows I have an adventurous spirit. I like to get off the main road and explore alternate routes. I call these detours "shortcuts." The problem is, we usually get lost. That's about the time the kids look out the window and ask, "Where are we?"

Barbie replies, "Dad is taking another one of his *longcuts*."

Do you really want to know why Moses and the people of Israel wandered in the wilderness for forty years? Because even back then men wouldn't stop and ask for directions!

Here's my point: We're spiritually and morally lost. What is truth and where can we find it? God speaks from Mount Sinai, giving us an ageless message to guide us. We don't need a new morality but an old one—inscribed in stone and written on our hearts. God says, "Stand at the crossroads and look; ask for the ancient paths, ask where the good way is, and walk in it, and you will find rest for your souls" (Jeremiah 6:16). Tragically, when Jeremiah gave this challenge, the people said, "We will not walk in it."

A famous skiing champion attempted a very difficult ski jump. The skier appeared in good form as he headed down the jump, but then, for no apparent reason, he tumbled head over heels off the side of the jump, bouncing off the supporting structure. Those who witnessed the apparent tragedy didn't know he chose to fall rather than finish the jump. He later explained the jump surface had become too fast, and midway down, he realized if he completed the jump, he would land on the level ground, beyond the safe landing area, which could have been fatal. As a result of a wise decision, he suffered only a headache from the tumble. The Ten Commandments challenges us to change our course in life before we experience a fatal landing.

Jesus said we can take the broad road that leads to destruction, or we can take the narrow road that leads to life. This narrow road is the road of faith and obedience to the commandments of God. Aleksandr Solzhenitsyn said, "One word of truth outweighs the whole world."

2
GET GOD BACK

"You shall have no other gods before me."

Exodus 20:3

The television commercial opened with the scene of a downtown crowded street featuring standstill traffic, horns blaring, a jackhammer pounding, and a cab driver shouting at the driver in front of him who was impeding his progress. The sidewalks were crowded with people shoving each other to get to work on time.

Then, a pencil with an eraser appeared on the screen. Slowly, it started erasing each part of the scene. First the cars, then the jackhammer, and then the taxicab. Each image, along with its accompanying sound, was erased until only one car remained—the newest car model being advertised. Finally, the word *SIMPLICITY* appeared on the screen.

Simplicity is the need of the hour. The one benefit of the global pandemic of Covid-19 taught us the power of simplicity. While great harm came from the pandemic, it also made us stop and return to a simpler life. Corporations are downsizing. We shop more online. We use telecommunication. We work from home, so we have more time with family and friends.

Just as we need a simple lifestyle, we need simplicity in our faith and values. The subject of morality is complex. Many viewpoints about what is right and what is wrong are advocated. Is there a simple code of ethics we can live by? Yes—the Ten Commandments give us ethical guidelines for a great life.

Where does morality come from? Morality comes from religion. Religion gives us our moral convictions. Historian Will Durant said, "No civilized society has ever been able to survive in history without a strong moral code. Nor has there ever been a moral code that was not formed by religion."

New Morality

It makes sense, then, that the Ten Commandments begins with God telling us, "You shall have no other gods before Me." Without God, morality cannot exist. The existence of the Law tells us there is a Lawgiver, and His truth is absolute. When we lose the knowledge of God, we lose our moral compass. God said, "My people have forgotten me, days without number" (Jeremiah 2:32).

Today, a new morality without God is on the rise. We need to get God back at the center of our lives. Let's talk about religion and why we need it. True religion is a personal relationship with God himself. His law is an expression of His love for us.

Most religions share three characteristics: beliefs, a code of conduct, and worship. Religion comes down to our concept of God and His will for our lives. Then, how we think about God shapes our attitudes, values, beliefs, philosophy of life, and, ultimately, our behavior. Rene

Descartes said, "I think; therefore, I am." Solomon concluded, "As [a man] thinks in his heart, so is he" (Proverbs 23:7 NKJV). Thinking determines living; especially, the way we think about God.

Reinhold Niebuhr said, "Irreligion is a luxury which only those may allow themselves who observe life rather than live it. Those who live [genuinely] must base their life upon an act of faith that life has meaning and seek to conform their actions to that meaning."[6]

The first commandment teaches us to think right about God: *You shall have no other gods before Me.* This command corrects false concepts of God. The first commandment refutes atheism, which says there is no God. It refutes agnosticism, which says God cannot be known. It refutes pantheism, which says God is a cosmic force that exists in everything. It refutes polytheism, which believes in multiple deities. It refutes humanism, which asserts humankind is the sum of all things.

God Out of Focus

Healthy living starts with understanding God as He really is. Only then will we be free of distorted images of God. Spiritual perception, just like good eyesight, is critically important. If we are spiritually blind, we will fall into a ditch, as Jesus said.

My son David Paul got his first pair of eyeglasses when he was three years old. An eye exam revealed he was extremely farsighted. I'll never forget the day we went to pick up his new glasses. Standing in the store, I put the glasses on him, and he opened his eyes as big as

---

[6] Quoted in *Christian Clippings* (Aug. 1997), 17.

saucers. He jerked the glasses off and said, "Dad, everything is so big!"

"Put them back on, son," I replied. "For the first time in your life you're seeing the world the way it really looks."

Many people don't understand God as He really is. They are spiritually farsighted. When you put on the glasses of the Bible, you'll know God. Any portrait of God, apart from the God of the Bible, is inadequate and distorted. The wrong image of God weakens our moral code. A. W. Tozer, in *The Knowledge of the Holy*, writes, "It is impossible to keep our moral practices sound and our inward attitudes right while our ideas about God are erroneous and inadequate."[7]

Your God Is Too Small

Ninety percent of American adults say they believe in God. But what kind of God? In *Your God Is Too Small*, J. B. Phillips says, "The trouble with many people today is that they have not found a God big enough for modern needs."[8] Phillips helps us see our weird ideas about God. Some people see God as the *Resident Policeman* who invokes feelings of fear and guilt. God, for others, is the *Parental Hangover*. He plays the same role our parents play in our lives.

Many people think of God as the *Grand Old Man*. For them, God is irrelevant. Certain religious upbringing gives people the *Meek-and-Mild* picture of God portrayed in paintings of Jesus carrying a sheep on His shoulder. They lose sight of God's power and majesty.

---

[7] A. W. Tozer, *The Knowledge of the Holy* (Lincoln: Back to the Bible Broadcast, 1961), 6.

[8] J. B. Phillips, *Your God Is Too Small* (Macmillan Company, 1961), 7.

Then, there is the God of *Absolute Perfection*. This God demands that we be perfect. No mistakes. No sins. It's all-or-nothing with Him. He always wants more from us. Of course, since we never reach perfection, the very thought of God brings with it feelings of failure. That's why a lot of people give up on their faith.

Many people, especially in the church, struggle with what Phillips calls, *God-in-a Box*. They think only of God in terms of institutional religion. Religious tradition, rather than the truth of God in Scripture, shapes their view of God.

Then there is the *God of Bethel*. This is the God of legalism. We believe if we keep all the rules, God is obligated to us. We try to manipulate God by prayers, confessions, and good deeds.

Finally, there is *God without the Godhead*. We depersonalize God. Rather than calling Him Father, we refer to Him as the higher power. But God isn't a force; He's your Father!

God is love. We are the masterpiece of His creation. His love was shown most clearly when He gave His Son, Jesus, for us on the Cross. "God so loved the world that he gave his one and only Son" (John 3:16). That's the most important thing you can know about God—He loves you!

You don't have to do anything to earn God's love. It's unconditional. You don't have to show great faith, pray great prayers, live a perfect live, or do good works for God to love you. God loves you just the way you are. In fact, He made you like you are. God's love liberates those who receive His love. "How much more will those who receive God's abundant provision of grace and the gift of righteousness reign in life through . . . Jesus Christ!"

(Romans 5:17). God not only loves us—*He is love!* His love is constant. It never changes. His love is absolute, unalterable, and unchanging. His love never fails.

Invasion of Privacy

The command for us to have no other gods before Him requires our total commitment and an undivided heart of devotion to God. We love the Lord with all our heart, soul, and strength. When we know God loves us, it follows naturally that we will love Him in return. Loving God means obeying Him. "We love because he first loved us" (1 John 4:19).

We are rebellious by nature. We don't like to obey. We'd rather be in charge. We don't want anyone, including God, telling us how to live. God has the audacity to invade our privacy and personal freedom with His commandments. Our tendency to rebel against God is cured when we realize His law is the pathway to life. Your quality of life will not be diminished in any way by obeying God's commandments. Your life will be enriched greatly. God's law reflects His love for us and His desire for us to enjoy the best life has to offer. As Jesus said, "I have come that they may have life, and have it [more abundantly]" (John 10:10). The prophet Isaiah said, "If you are willing and obedient, you will eat the good things of the land" (Isaiah 1:19).

Submission to God's will is the secret of the good life everybody is searching for. The Biblical word for *worship* means "to bow down before God." Worship means surrendering ourselves to the will of God in total obedience. The first use of the word *worship* in the Bible occurs when

God told Abraham to give up his son Isaac as an offering. Despite all his unanswered questions, he set out in faith to the appointed place in obedience to God. God was testing his faith. Abraham's words to his servants stir the human soul: "Stay here with the donkey while I and the boy go over there. We will worship and then we will come back to you" (Genesis 22:5). We will come back! He knew God was testing his faith to reveal Himself as Jehovah Jireh, the Lord our provider. What faith! What obedience! What surrender!

Gottfried Silbermann built one of the greatest organs in the world and completed it in 1714 for the Freiburg Cathedral, where it is still in use today. One day, the renowned Felix Mendelssohn (1809-1847)—a musical prodigy, composer, pianist, and organist—visited the cathedral to see the magnificent Silbermann organ. Awed by its construction and sound, he asked the resident organist if he could play it. The organist refused his request at first but finally granted him permission.

As Mendelssohn began to play the organ with impeccable skill and precision, the thunder of the powerful organ filled the cathedral with a divine melody. It was as though there came a sound from Heaven. The organist stood in awe by the performance.

"What is your name?" he asked the visitor.

"Felix Mendelssohn," he replied.

The organist apologized and said, "Just think of it. The Master was here, and I almost refused to let him play this magnificent instrument."

Exclusive Love

The phrase *no other gods before Me* means "in hostility toward Me." Don't allow anything in your life to oppose God's rightful place. Be on your guard against any attitude, belief, or value that undermines your exclusive love for God. Jesus put it this way: "No one can serve two masters. Either you will hate the one and love the other, or you will be devoted to the one and despise the other. You cannot serve both God and money" (Matthew 6:24).

King Ahaz of Judah visited the Assyrian king of Damascus (2 Kings 16:10-16). During his time there, he noticed a pagan altar that impressed him. He had a copy of it constructed and put in the Temple in Jerusalem right next to God's altar. The altar of the Lord was used for prayer, while the pagan altar was used for sacrifice. His actions were intended to show his submission to Assyria, whom he feared.

He didn't remove God from his life, but he added a pagan god. He mixed true worship with pagan ritual. He wanted to be both spiritual and secular. He didn't want to get God out of his life; he still wanted to receive God's blessings. But now Ahaz's heart was divided. He tried to have it both ways. God wasn't enough for him; he had to have the world too.

God created us for an exclusive love relationship. The early church understood this truth. The creed of early believers was simply, "Jesus Christ is Lord." To follow Jesus means to forsake all others who would claim lordship over our life.

When Emperor Nero claimed to be divine and required all citizens of Rome to pledge their loyalty by declaring "Caesar is Lord," the Christians refused. They only acknowledged Jesus as Lord. They belonged exclusively to Jesus.

When Paul was imprisoned for his faith, he called himself "the prisoner of Christ Jesus" (Ephesians 3:1). He didn't call himself a prisoner of Rome or the prisoner of Caesar but the prisoner of the Lord. Jesus ruled on the throne of his heart, and to use Paul's words, "that Christ may dwell in your hearts through faith" (Ephesians 3:17).

One day a wealthy young man came to Jesus seeking eternal life. He asked, "What must I do to inherit eternal life?" He had it all—youth, wealth, and power. He was the envy of other young people in his day.

Jesus told him, "You know the commandments. Do not commit adultery, do not murder, do not steal, do not give false testimony, honor your father and mother." Jesus began with the Law to help him see his need of God's grace. The law of God makes us conscious of sin and leads us to the Savior.

The young man replied, "All these I have kept since I was a boy." I would've liked to have seen the expression on Jesus' face when he uttered such foolish words. What do you say to someone who thinks he's perfect? Obviously, he didn't know the spiritual condition of his own heart.

Jesus then got to the real issue: "You still lack one thing. Sell everything you have and give it to the poor, and you will have treasure in heaven. Then come, follow me" (Luke 18:22).

Sadly, the young man refused Jesus' invitation. He didn't refuse because he was wealthy. He rejected Christ because his wealth and position kept a strong grip on him. Jesus simply showed him that he hadn't kept all the commandments since his youth. In fact, he was in violation of the first command, "You shall have no other gods before me" (Exodus 20:3). Money was his god. Money and power reigned on the throne of his heart, making him so self-sufficient he couldn't let it go to gain Christ. His money and power kept him from following Jesus. He wasn't bound by what he possessed but rather by what possessed him.

How much better to live the words of the song, "I'd rather have Jesus than anything this world affords today." Paul gave up his pride and religion to gain Christ. "Whatever were gains to me, I now consider loss . . . so that I may gain Christ and be found in him, not having a righteousness of my own . . . but the righteousness that comes from God on the basis of faith. I want to know Christ" (Philippians 3:7, 10).

Why Worship?

Why do we worship God? This may shock you, but God doesn't need our love or worship. God enjoys our love and worship, but He doesn't need it. God is self-existent. He doesn't *need* anything. Worship is God's gift to us. We're the ones who need to worship. Worship brings us into the presence of God, where we find the fullness of joy.

We worship God because of who He is and because of what He has done for us. Listen again to the first commandment: "I am the Lord your God, who brought you out of Egypt, out of the land of slavery. You shall have no other gods before me" (Exodus 20:2-3). It is because God brought us out of the slavery of sin and set us free that we worship Him. True worship is our response of love to the love of God. We rejoice because we are redeemed. We boast because we are blessed. We celebrate because we are called. We sing because we are saved. We shout because we are sanctified. We have joy because we are justified. We have faith because we are forgiven. We are grateful because of grace. We are thankful because we are transformed. We love because we are liberated. That's why we worship our God in Spirit and in truth!

Redemption means purchasing something valuable at a high price. It also means setting someone from bondage. When people in the ancient world lost property because of financial hardship, another member of their family had the right to buy the property back if they could pay the full price and clear the family from debt. God redeemed Israel from slavery in Egypt by his power marked by ten judgments, the Red Sea miracle, and the atoning blood of the Passover lamb. We are purchased by the life of Jesus, and He sets us free to serve him! The theme of redemption is the silver thread woven through every nook and cranny of the Bible, telling us the story of God's amazing grace.

Jesus fulfilled the Old Testament acts of redemption, the most important being the Passover that took place in Egypt. Passover is celebrated every year in the Jewish faith. The Jewish holy day of Yom Kippur, the Day of Atonement, is also celebrated every year, which was fulfilled in Jesus' death on the cross, for "He is the atoning sacrifice for our sins, and not only for ours but also for the sins of the whole world" (1 John 2:2). The redemptive stories and festivals point to Jesus. "Christ, our Passover lamb, has been sacrificed" (1 Corinthians 5:7). John the Baptist introduced Jesus to the world. "Look, the Lamb of God, who takes away the sins of the world!" (John 1:29).

The Apostle Peter assures us, "For you know that it was not with perishable things such as silver or gold that you were redeemed from the empty way of life . . . but with the precious blood of Christ, a lamb without blemish or defect" (1 Peter 1:18-19). What a great salvation! What a reason to worship God!

The Apostle Paul asked, "Do you not know that your bodies are temples of the Holy Spirit, who is in you, whom you have received from God? You are not your own; you were bought at a price" (1 Corinthians 6:19-20).

That's what redemption means—you were bought at the high price of the precious blood of Christ. So, you are not your own. You belong to God. Therefore, glorify God with your life. "So, whether you eat or drink or whatever you do, do it all for the glory of God" (10:31).

When making moral decisions, we should ask the preeminent question: Does it glorify God? If it does, we have liberty to do it. If it does not, we avoid it because we are redeemed and we belong to Him.

Christian morality is more about desire than discipline. Obedience to God comes from our love for Him, not our fear of Him. Love and obedience go hand in hand. "We know that we have come to know him if we [obey] his commands" (1 John 2:3).

Put Your World Together

He came home from work one evening exhausted after a long day at work. Relaxing in his favorite chair, he turned on the football game featuring his favorite team. His little boy jumped into his lap and said, "Daddy, let's play!"

Dad didn't feel like playing, so he tried to get his son occupied doing something. He noticed a full-page ad in the newspaper lying on the table with a picture of the earth taken from space. He told his son to get a pair of scissors and some scotch tape. He proceeded to cut up the picture of the world into a lot of small pieces, making a jigsaw puzzle. He handed the pieces of paper to his son along with the scotch tape and told him, "Go put the pieces back together and make the picture of the world. Then, come show it to me."

The man thought that would keep the boy occupied while he watched the game on TV.

Ten minutes later, his son jumped into his lap holding up the completed picture.

"Look, Daddy, I put it back together."

Shocked, his father said, "How did you put all the pieces back together so quickly?"

The boy turned the picture of the world over. "Look Daddy, on the back side there's a picture of a man. When I put the man together, the whole world came together."

God gave us His grace in Christ to put us back together. He writes His law on our hearts to keep us together in a world that has lost its moral compass. All of life comes together when we obey the first commandment: *You shall have no other gods before Me.*

3
A JEALOUS GOD

*"You shall not make for yourselves an idol . . . for I,
the Lord your God, am a jealous God."*
Exodus 20:4, 6

Image is everything, or so the advertising world thinks. Advertisers entice us to buy eye-appealing goods so we can look the best, have the best, and be the best. Images are designed to make us want products. We are also very image-conscious. Selfies and social media have made us more self-aware and conscious of our appearance because we constantly look at ourselves. We constantly manage our image.

A young businessman I knew in Atlanta told me how he got himself into financial jeopardy. He got into debt by financing an image of success with an expensive car, expensive suits, and dining at the best restaurants to impress his potential clients. He tried to buy an image of success rather than achieving success the proper way. He told me, "I had to have all of this stuff in order to do business." He should have focused on achieving success rather than trying to look successful to impress others.

It's easy to focus on self-image and forget about character development. Many people project an image of happiness, success, and even wealth, but their lives tell a different story. I overheard a man tell his friend, "I can't believe you got divorced. You guys looked so happy together."

He replied with disappointment, "It was all an image we put on to impress others."

Image and reality are two different things. This brings up the issue of faith. Do we really know God? Do we trust Him regardless of the circumstances? Do we really love and serve Him? Is our faith more image than reality? Some people pretend to be religious, but they don't really know God.

The second commandment forbids idolatry: *You shall not make for yourselves an idol in the form of anything.* God doesn't want us to have an image of faith. He wants us to experience Him in real life. Since the beginning of time, humanity has been guilty of making idols. Ancient idols still exist around the world. Even in our age of technology we have idols. They may not be the rough, crude hand-carved images made of wood and stone, but they're still idols.

While on a preaching trip in South India, I had an experience with primitive idolatry. After one service, we took a rickshaw back to our hotel. That night, in the town square, there was a loud commotion. The night sky was lit up by torches being carried by a crowd. They were dancing around a large, ancient idol being pulled on a wooden cart by a couple of men. As the crowd danced wildly, they chanted loudly to the image of a false god.

What a tragic scene: well-meaning people, chanting to an idol in a land of abject poverty and suffering! Their god could do nothing to help them out of their poverty and superstition. The idol was an image of power but was totally powerless. The idol couldn't hear their chants and prayers to help them. The connection between their idol and their suffering was crystal clear to me.

We often hear that politics has consequences. Well, so does religion. It has negative consequences when it is based on spiritual error and unbiblical doctrines. A misguided faith leads to a misdirected life.

Idols in the Heart

Is that all there is to idolatry? Primitive people worshiping images of wood and stone? If so, then we're off the hook. After all, ours is the day of philosophical enlightenment, information technology, and scientific advancement. We don't have idols . . . or do we?

The fact is that images made of wood, stone, or precious metals aren't idols at all. These are merely outward images of idolatrous ideas of God. Real idols exist in the heart. God told Ezekiel, "Son of man, these men have set up idols in their hearts and put wicked stumbling blocks before their faces. Should I let them inquire of me at all?" (Ezekiel 14:3). The phrase "idols in their hearts" leaps off the page of the Bible. All idols are really idols of the heart.

The Bible gives more warnings against idolatry than anything else. Moses cautioned Israel, "Be careful, or you will be enticed to turn away and worship other gods and bow down to them" (Deuteronomy 11:16).

While King Solomon experienced an unsurpassed measure of God's wisdom, he failed to guard his heart in this area. The result was tragic: "As Solomon grew old, his wives turned his heart after other gods, and his heart was not fully devoted to the Lord his God, as the heart of David his father had been" (1 Kings 11:4).

The prophet Jeremiah gives us an unmistakable picture of the futility of idolatry: "Like a scarecrow in a cucumber field, their idols cannot speak; they must be carried because they cannot walk. Do not fear them; they can do no harm nor can they do any good" (Jeremiah 10:5).

I visited the Acropolis in Athens, Greece, where Paul delivered an address to a group of philosophers at Mars Hill. When he arrived in Athens, he quickly noticed how idolatrous the city was. He told the people, "Since we are God's offspring, we should not think that the divine being is like gold or silver or stone—an image made by human design" (Acts 17:29). Then he noticed a statue made to "The Unknown God," and he proceeded to tell them about the true and living God. We, too, live in a world of idols. So, the apostle John cautions us, "Dear children, keep yourselves from idols" (1 John 5:21).

Now, let's clear up one matter before we go any further. Some might misconstrue these verses forbidding idolatry to imply that other gods exist. The "gods" we are forbidden to worship aren't real. They are illusions, existing only in the mind. "We know that 'An idol is nothing at all in the world' and that 'There is no God but one.' For even if there are so-called gods, whether in heaven or on earth . . . yet for us there is but one God, the Father, from whom all things came and for whom we live; and there is but one Lord, Jesus Christ, through whom all things came and through whom we live" (1 Corinthians 8:4-6).

Taking God's Place

Idolatry is anything man worships in the place of God. Idols are distorted images of God's true nature as revealed in the Bible. The Greek word for *idol* refers to that which is unreal and empty. Plato used the word *idol* to refer to the illusions of the world that stand in contrast to truths.

So, an idol is anything that takes the place of God. Idols are illusions and lead to a life of emptiness. The command to not make an idol in the form of anything doesn't apply to art, painting, sculptures and so forth. Art isn't a graven image that we worship in the place of God. Sacred art is an image to God's glory that inspires us to worship the Lord.

Art is not idolatry. We admire art and it inspires us, but we don't worship art. The act of making a graven image means to refashion God that is contrary to the way He has revealed Himself to us in nature, history, the Bible, and in Jesus Christ. Our culture is reimaging God instead of reverencing God. The new God of the age is a God of tolerance not truth, who is ever-evolving rather than never-changing, and who is all-permissible rather than all-powerful.

God is Creator. The revelation of God in Scripture begins with our full acceptance and belief in one paramount fact: "In the beginning God created the heavens and the earth" (Genesis 1:1). God exists within Himself as self-sustaining. God is the sole originator of the universe and the author of life. "For from him and through him and for him are all things. To him be the glory forever! Amen" (Romans 11:36).

God is providential. "The earth is the Lord's and everything in it" (Psalm 24:1). God holds the universe together, "sustaining all things by His powerful word" (Hebrews 1:3). He causes the planets to rotate in order. He sustains the laws of physics and chemistry. He maintains the delicate balance of oxygen, nitrogen, and other gases sustaining life on earth. God causes the heart to beat, the lungs to breathe, and the brain to send impulses to the body's vital organs. God causes the sun to rise as the morning brings us word of His unfailing love. "Now to the King eternal, immortal, invisible, the only God, be honor and glory for ever and ever. Amen" (1 Timothy 1:17).

God is Savior. God delivers His people from the presence and power of sin. "Where sin increased, grace increased all the more" (Romans 5:20). God is a God of infinite forgiveness, who comes to our aid when we call on Him and delivers us from all our troubles. "The Lord lives! Praise be to my Rock! Exalted be God my Savior!" (Psalm 18:46).

God cares about us. God is not watching us from a distance. He is present and active in our lives. Jesus said God knows when a sparrow falls to the ground, and He has numbered the hairs on our heads. So, "Cast your anxiety on him because he cares for you" (1 Peter 5:7).

God is revealed in Jesus Christ. The full revelation of God is seen in Jesus Christ. He is the "image of the invisible God" (Colossians 1:15), "the radiance of God's glory and the exact representation of his being" (Hebrews 1:3). "No one has ever seen God, but the one and only Son, who is himself God and is in closest relationship with the Father, has made him known" (John 1:18). The only accurate portrait of God you will ever see is Jesus. When Jesus was born, He was given the name *Emmanuel,* meaning, "God with us."

The Apostle John wrote, "In the beginning was the Word, and the Word was with God, and the Word was God" (v. 1). He continued, "The Word became flesh and made his dwelling among us. We have seen his glory, the glory of the one and only Son, who came from the Father, full of grace and truth" (v. 14).

Why did John refer to Jesus as "the Word"? The Greek word is *logos.* This was a very important word in the ancient world. *Logos* to the Hebrew mind was the word that described God himself. It spoke of God as Creator. It was also used to describe God's work of mediation or atonement for humanity's sin. *Logos,* then, is the bridge between God and man. The Greeks used the word *logos* to speak of the organizing intelligence behind creation and the sustaining power of the universe. They also used *logos* to describe the bridge between God and man, like a priest. *Logos* to the Greeks was the sum of absolute truth.

You can see why John used the word *logos* to describe Jesus. He was saying to the people of his time: Do you want to know who created the world? Do you want to understand the power that holds the universe together? Do you want to comprehend the organizing, intellectual power behind creation? Do you want to know the way to God, the bridge between God and man? Look at Jesus. He is the *logos* of God. He is the revelation of God.

We will see God clearly only when we see Him in the face of Jesus, who said, "Anyone who has seen me he has seen the Father" (John 14:9).

Substitutes for God

Idols comes in all shapes and sizes. People substitute things for God. I always enjoyed having a substitute teacher at school because they didn't make us do much work. They were more lenient than the real teacher. Israel substituted a golden calf for God. Nebuchadnezzar substituted a gold statue 75 feet high in the place of God. Religious leaders in Jesus' day substituted tradition for truth. The rich young ruler who came to Christ substituted wealth for obedience. Demas, a young man who started his ministry with Paul, substituted love for the world in God's place.

After King Solomon's death, civil war broke out in Israel. The ten tribes in the north formed the nation of Israel. The two tribes in the south formed the nation of Judah. The rebel king of the northern empire, Jeroboam, set up a new capital in Samaria along with a new temple. He did this so the Jews would not go back to the Temple in Jerusalem to worship. He wanted to sever their relationship with Jehovah God. He also built two golden calves and placed them in the cities of Bethel and Dan. If this wasn't enough to destroy the nation's faith, he built high places where the people could offer sacrifices. He also established his own priesthood to rival the Levitical priesthood. Every Israelite king who followed Jeroboam was ungodly and engaged in idol worship, eventually leading to the nation's defeat by the army of Assyria in 722 B C.

Jeroboam didn't come right out and tell the people not to worship the true and living God. He gave them substitutes for God—a golden calf, a new temple, and a new priesthood. He copied the form of worship but abandoned the heart of worship. As the years passed in Israel, their memory of God, His redemptive acts, and His sacred word faded from their minds. We see the same trend today in America as we become less sacred and more secular, less Christian, and more cultural.

The Supreme Court of Alabama once tried a case to decide whether a judge could display the Ten Commandments in his courtroom. There was a day in America where a bogus lawsuit of such nature would be thrown out of court without legal merit. Aleksandr Solzhenitsyn said, "The greatest tragedy that can befall a nation is the tragedy of forgetting God."

During a television interview, Dr. Alveda King pointed out the omission of the President when he failed to mention the name of God in the National Day of Prayer proclamation. She asked, "How can you be the President of the United States and not use the word *God* in the national call to prayer?" She went on to remind the audience that our national motto is, "One nation under God" and our currency reads, "In God We Trust."

God himself will be the final target of cancel culture. God is often omitted from our thoughts, plans, relationships, businesses, schools, politics and even in some religions. God laments, "Yet my people have forgotten me, days without number" (Jeremiah 2:32). Can we have prayer without God? If we omit God, to whom or what are we praying? Can we have faith without God? Who or what do we believe in if we omit God? The power is not in prayer or in faith but in God! Jesus said, "Have faith in God" (Mark 11:22). We don't turn to prayer for hope;

we look to the living God as our Creator, Redeemer, and Father.

At the funeral of Louis XIV, the cathedral was packed with mourners paying tribute to the great monarch they all revered. The sanctuary was dark, except for one solitary candle which illuminated the great casket which held his remains. Massillon, the minister overseeing the service, stood to address the crowd. He reached his hand around the pulpit and snuffed out the solitary candle which had been lit to honor the great king. His voice declared these solemn words in the darkness, "God only is great!"

Additions to God

Idolatry can also take the form of adding something to God. During my travels to India, I had dinner with a wealthy Hindu businessman at his home. After dinner he invited me to see his private shrine. He led me into a small room about the size of a walk-in closet. The walls were lined with shelves filled with small idols to various Hindu deities. He took a figurine of Mary holding the infant Jesus off a shelf and proudly showed it to me.

"Look," he said with a big smile on his face, "I even have the Christian God, Jesus."

My heart broke. I knew he was only doing what he had been taught. So, I took time to share with him why Jesus is greater than all other gods. In fact, He alone is God.

This businessman's religion was the idolatry of "God and _____." Sometimes idolatry involves worshiping God while, at the same time, having unholy affections toward things that are hostile to Him.

King Joash of Judah gave God incomplete obedience. The Bible commends him because "he did what was right in the eyes of the Lord." That's the good news. Now for the bad news: "But he did not remove the high places." These high places were pagan altars to false gods where the people continued to offer sacrifices and burn incense (see 2 Kings 12:1-21).

Joash didn't go far enough in his spiritual reforms. The high places continued to occupy a place in Israel's worship in hostility to God's supreme place in their lives. Are there any high places in your life? If so, remove all the high places and serve the Lord with all your heart, soul, and strength.

What Idolatry Costs

Idolatry is costly. Israel learned this lesson the hard way. After Joshua died, "another generation grew up, who knew neither the Lord nor what he had done for Israel." The result was tragic: "Then the Israelites did evil in the eyes of the Lord and served the Baals" (Judges 2:10-11).

The spiritual downfall of Israel started with the lack of Biblical education—another generation grew up, who didn't know the Lord or what he had done for them. They didn't know about God and his great works, nor did they have a personal relationship with Him and personal reverence for Him. Their ignorance led to immorality—they did evil in the eyes of the Lord. They abandoned the moral principles of Scripture and conformed to the pagan culture of Canaan. Finally, they fell into idolatry—they served the Baals. Many years later, the great prophet Elijah defeated the false prophets of Baal and removed the idols from Israel.

In America, Biblical illiteracy is at an all-time high. We are following the same path as ancient Israel.

We become what we worship. If we worship money, we become materialists. If we worship pleasure, we become hedonists. If we worship power, we manipulate others. If we worship fame, we become little gods. If we worship the self, we become narcissists. However, if we worship God in Spirit and in truth, we become like Him. We "[reflect like] a mirror the glory of the Lord" (2 Corinthians 3:18 NKJV).

Selfies

The greatest idolatry is the idolatry of the self. Pride is the essence of sin. Sin exalts the desires of the self above the place of God and the needs of others, resulting in a life of self-interest and self-indulgence.

Narcissism is a major psychological disorder of our day. It derives its name from the Greek mythological character Narcissus, who was the son of Cephalus, the river god. He would sit for hours gazing at the reflection of his own image in a pool. He loved himself so much that he rejected the love of the nymph Echo. He even spurned associations with his friends. One day he leaned over to kiss his own reflection and drowned in the pool.

Narcissism is self-absorption. It differs somewhat from egotism. The egotist doesn't care what people think about him. He sees the world as a place to be conquered. However, the narcissist cares deeply about what others think. He is on a quest to discover himself. He needs constant affirmation and attention. Without it, he becomes depressed or even paranoid. He is overly dependent on the opinion and approval of others, feels desperately insecure, and is overly concerned with his public image.

The narcissist projects an image of self-confidence while being plagued by feelings of inadequacy. He is obsessed with what this person meant by what he said or what this event means to him. The narcissist searches constantly for more out of everything—more personal meaning, more out of relationships, more out of work, more out of the church, more out of marriage. Narcissists are rarely content because they are driven to get more and are seldom grateful for what they have.

The narcissist lives for the moment, with little or no concern for the historical past or the future. His primary motivation in every endeavor or relationship is, *What am I getting out of it?* Narcissism is self-worship. It is based on what the self wants rather than what God says or what others need.[9] And that's exactly how many people decide what's right and wrong. The self, not God, is at the center of their world.

One day Savonarola, a fifteenth-century preacher, noticed an elderly woman worshiping before a statue of the Virgin Mary. The statue stood in a great cathedral. Time and time again he had seen her on her knees before this statue. He commented to a friend on one occasion, "Look how she reveres the Virgin Mary."

"Don't be deceived by what you see," his friend replied. "Many years ago, an artist was commissioned to create a statue for the cathedral. He selected that woman in her youthful beauty and innocence for a model. Shortly after the statue was put in place, she began to visit it and has worshiped there religiously ever since."

---

[9] Roy K. McClaughry, *The Eye of the Needle* (Leicester: Inter-Varsity Press, 1990), 31-33.

A Jealous God

God reveals something very special about Himself in this commandment to not make idols. He says, "I am a jealous God." That's an odd statement for God to make. Shakespeare called jealousy the "green-eyed monster."

Jealousy is an intense emotion which can take the positive form of zeal and passion or the negative form of envy. The Hebrew word *jealous* means "to become red," describing the color of the human face when experiencing this emotion. The Greek word means "to boil."

God is jealous because He alone deserves to be worshiped and obeyed (see Exodus 34:14). God's jealousy is provoked by idolatry (Isaiah 59:17-18). He is jealous for us because He loves us. "The Lord Almighty says: 'I am very jealous for Jerusalem and Zion'" (Zechariah 1:14). God is "a consuming fire" who loves us with an all-consuming love (Hebrews 12:29).

The Book of James helps us understand the jealousy of God. James wrote, "He [God] yearns jealously over the spirit that he has made to dwell in us" (4:5 ESV). It can also mean "The Spirit who dwells in us yearns jealously" (NKJV). When the human spirit is touched by the Holy Spirit, we are drawn by God's love into a life of devotion. This is what Elijah meant when he prayed, "I have been very zealous for the Lord God Almighty" (1 Kings 19:10).

Guest or Family?

The Apostle Paul described the deep personal relationship we can have with the Lord: "I pray that . . . Christ may dwell in your hearts through faith" (Ephesians 3:16-17). The word *dwell* means "to be at home at or to take up permanent residence." Jesus is only an occasional visitor in some people's hearts. But Jesus desires to make his permanent home within us. We need to sign over the deed of our hearts to Jesus, so He is Lord over every aspect of our lives.

We've all experienced unexpected guests who call us and say they're going to stop by the house and visit. The problem is, we're not ready for them! The house is a mess. So, what do we do? We run through the house hiding everything we can, wherever we can, as fast as we can. We throw things in the closets and the bedrooms, shut the doors, tidy up a few things, and greet them at the front door with a big smile.

They walk in, look around and say, "Your home is so lovely! I wish our house looked this nice all the time." If they only knew the truth. Although we tell them, "Make yourself at home," we don't really mean it. We don't want them to *dwell* with us. A guest stays in their designated area. They don't see the messy bedrooms or closets. We hide the mess, so they only see the masterpiece. They only see the parts of the house we allow them to see. We make our homes presentable for guests but livable for us!

Jesus doesn't want to visit our hearts; he wants to live in us. That's what it means "that Christ will dwell in your hearts by faith." Does He dwell with you? Is He at home in your heart? Do you allow Him to go into the closets of bitterness, resentment, and sin and clean up the mess? Is He welcome to go into the attic of your mind and the basement of your beliefs to transform your thinking so you live by the mind of Christ? Jesus said, "If anyone loves Me, he will keep My word; and My Father will love him, and We will come to him and make Our home with him" (John 14:23 NKJV).

When Michelangelo was painting or sculpting a great work of art, he would close himself off from the outside world. A friend asked him, "Why do you lead such a solitary life?"

"Art," he replied, "is a jealous god; it requires the whole and entire artist."

During the years he painted the Sistine Chapel, he avoided social gatherings and talking to friends for long periods of time to devote his time to his art. He didn't want to get distracted from his work so he could do his very best.

This is what Paul meant when he wrote, "I am afraid that just as Eve was deceived by the serpent's cunning, your minds may somehow be led astray from your sincere and pure devotion to Christ" (2 Corinthians 11:3).

I had the privilege of growing up in church from the time I was born. I've always enjoyed going to church, and especially the music. The greatest music in the world is heard in Christian churches. I've always been inspired by the melody and lyrics of the hymn, "Take My Life and Let It Be." The song became a heartfelt prayer as a young boy from my heart to Christ to this very day:

> *Take my life, and let it be*
> *Consecrated, Lord, to Thee;*
> *Take my moments and my days,*
> *Let them flow in ceaseless praise.*
>
> *Take my will and make it Thine.*
> *It shall be no longer mine.*
> *Take my heart; it is Thine own.*
> *It shall be Thy royal throne.*

Take my love; my Lord, I pour
At Thy feet its treasure-store.
Take myself, and I will be
Ever, only, all for Thee,
Ever, only, all for Thee.

4
NOTHING SACRED

"You shall not misuse the name of the Lord your God."
Exodus 20:7

The interviewer asked a comedian who starred in a weekly television comedy, "What makes your show such a big success?"

He replied, "Our program is successful because we consider nothing sacred."

Sometimes we get the feeling that dishonoring the sacred has become the order of the day. Have we indeed entered a time in American history when absolutely nothing is sacred?

The prophet Daniel was exiled to Babylon during the Jewish captivity. One evening Belshazzar, king of Babylon, hosted a royal party. When the party reached its peak of debauchery, he ordered that the holy articles from the Temple in Jerusalem be brought out so the guests could use them. Belshazzar profaned the holy vessels, using them as they were not sacred, and God's judgment was the result.

The party ended abruptly when the hand of God appeared writing a mysterious message on the palace wall:

Mene Tekel, Uparsin. None of the king's wise men could interpret it. So, Daniel was summoned to interpret the strange message. His interpretation pronounced God's judgment against Babylon:

> *Mene:* God has numbered the days of your reign and brought it to an end.
>
> *Tekel:* You have been weighed on the scales and found wanting.
>
> *Uparsin:* Your kingdom is divided and given to the Medes and Persians.

Shortly after the handwriting on the wall, Belshazzar's kingdom fell to the kingdom of Medo-Persia. King Belshazzar was a man to whom not even the holy articles from the Temple of God were sacred. We need a sense of awe about sacred things. God instructed the Levitical priests to "distinguish between the holy and the [profane], between the unclean and the clean" (Leviticus 10:10). So must we.

Crossroads Connection

In Lewis Carroll's classic *Alice in Wonderland,* Alice comes to a fork in the road. Confused, she asks the Cheshire Cat which road to take.

"Where do you want to go?" asked the Cat.

Alice replied, "I don't know."

"Then," said the Cat, "it doesn't matter which way you go."

Which way do we want to go? Spiritual or secular? Will we follow Christ or culture? Will we choose the ancient path of spirituality or the new road of secularism? Is God relevant or an outdated belief that once had benefit but is no longer needed?

While America has never been Christian in the sense that every citizen confessed Jesus as Lord, the foundations of our democracy were formed by Biblical ethics. Supreme Court Chief Justice Earl Warren underscored the role the Christian faith plays in the success of the American dream in a speech delivered on February 4, 1954 in Washington, D.C.

> I believe no one can read the history of our country without realizing that the Good Book and the spirit of the Savior have from the beginning been our guiding genius. . . . Whether we look to the first Charter of Virginia, or to the Charter of New England, or to the Charter of Massachusetts Bay, or to the Fundamental Orders of Connecticut, the same objective is present: a Christian land governed by Christian principles. I believe the entire Bill of Rights came into being because of the knowledge our forefathers had of the Bible and their belief in it: freedom of belief, or expression, of assembly, of petition, the dignity of the individual, the sanctity of the home, equal justice under law, and the reservation of powers to the people. . . . I like to believe we are living today in the spirit of the Christian religion. I like also to believe that if we do so, no great harm can come to our country.[10]

Life Without God

Such high and lofty values, rooted in the absolute morality of Scripture, provides a sense of *transcendence*. Transcendence means to live with an awareness of the existence and providence of God. God is above and beyond us. His law is eternal and absolute.

---

[10] *ourlostfounding.com*

Historically, nations lose this sense of transcendence when they move in one of two directions: materialism or spiritualism. Material prosperity alone doesn't bring fulfillment. We feel spiritually empty, and long for a greater purpose in life than merely achieving wealth. Material possessions cannot meet our deepest spiritual and emotional needs. Unfortunately, many are turning to new gods to fill the spiritual void left by materialism.

Selfism is the new religion of the day. Instead of looking up to Heaven, selfism says we should look within ourselves. Selfism deludes us into believing we are gods and self-determining creatures. Deep ecology is gaining ground in our culture. We celebrate Earth Day but disregard the Lord's Day. Mother Earth, called Gaia, is seen by some as a deity who is the source of life. Spiritual feminism says God is really a goddess with feminine qualities that must replace the violent, competitive, patriarchal style that dominates the marketplace. Ecology, for some, has become idolatry.

Humanity is still trying to build the city of man without the city of God, as Augustine, the early church leader, observed. Can it be done? Nineteenth century novelist Dostoevsky asked in his classic work, *Brothers Karamazov*, "Can man live without God?" Then he said, "If God does not exist, everything else is permissible."

When British statesman Lord Gladstone was asked if there was anything that frightened him about the future, he replied, "Yes, one thing; the fear that God seems to be dying out in the minds of men."

Such was the concern of the prophet Jeremiah. He challenged his generation, "Has a nation ever changed its gods? (Yet they are not gods at all.) But my people have exchanged their glorious God for worthless idols. . . . Does a young woman forget her jewelry, a bride her wedding ornaments? Yet my people have forgotten me, days without number" (Jeremiah 2:11, 32). God speaks to our generation that has forgotten Him and says, *You shall not misuse the name of the Lord your God.*

What I appreciate most about the Ten Commandments is their forthrightness. A local community newspaper editor ran a copy of the Ten Commandments in his column without citing the source. One angry reader wrote the editor to demand, "I want you to cancel my subscription to your paper. You're getting too personal."

What does it mean to misuse God's name? It means to take God's name in vain. The name of God describes who He is. The ancient Hebrews thought of a name as the representation of a person. The Hebrew word translated *misuse* or *take in vain* means to treat it in a way that has no value. *Misuse* literally means to treat the name of God as irrelevant. People misuse God's name because He doesn't mean anything to them. It is a great act of irreverence toward God.

God is called by several names in the Old Testament. Each one shows us something about who He is. God is called *Elohim*, the Creator, the Faithful One who commits himself to us by an unbreakable oath or promise. He is *El Olam*, the everlasting God. He is *El Shaddai*, literally, the God of the mountains, who is the Almighty. He is the all-sufficient God who provides for His people. El-Shaddai has a feminine quality referring to a mother nursing her children. God is called *Adonai*, meaning Lord, Ruler, and Sovereign King—the Lord of all lords and the God of all so-called gods.

God's most sacred name is *Yahweh,* or *Jehovah.* The name Jehovah appears over 6,000 times in the Old Testament. Jehovah is the covenant name of God. It really means "the Promise Keeper." God gave Israel this name to teach them He is faithful to His promises. The name *Jehovah* is written as LORD, with small capital letters, in English Bibles.

The name *Jehovah* appears 162 times in Genesis. It was first given by God to Moses at the famous burning bush. God told Moses to deliver Israel from Egyptian slavery. Moses objected and asked, "Who shall I say sent me?" God responded, "I am who I am" (Exodus 3:14). It means, "I will be what I will be." God was telling Moses, "I will be what you need in every situation you face."

The name of Jehovah is fulfilled in the name *Jesus,* meaning "the Lord saves." Paul declared, "Therefore God exalted him to the highest place and gave him the name that is above every name, that at the name of Jesus every knee should bow, in heaven and on earth and under the earth, and every tongue acknowledge that Jesus Christ is Lord, to the glory of God the Father" (Philippians 2:9-11).

Any way we look at it, the name of the Lord is sacred. When we speak His name, we are declaring our faith in Him, our love for Him, and our loyalty to Him.

Watch Your Words

The name of the Lord is used so irreverently. Profanity is the most obvious way God's name is misused. The name of God has become a common swear word. The word *profanity* comes from two Latin words, *pro* meaning "in front of"; and *fane,* meaning "temple." A profane word, then, is a word that no one would speak in a temple or in a church. The free-flowing profanity of our day is clear evidence that nothing is sacred. Not even the name of God himself.

We also misuse God's name when we curse others. "With the tongue we praise our Lord and Father, and with it we curse human beings, who have been made in God's likeness. Out of the same mouth come praise and cursing. My brothers, this should not be" (James 3:9-10). Words spoken in rage, hatred, and discrimination toward others, who are made in God's image, are words spoken against the Creator. As Proverbs 12:18 says, "Words of the reckless pierce like swords, but the tongue of the wise brings healing." If we took this commandment seriously, it would end abusive language toward others and the meaningless profanity that has become so common.

Accusing God of doing wrong is another way we misuse His name. The account of Job's suffering is almost universally known. Despite intense personal pain, overwhelming loss, and unanswered questions, "In all this, Job did not sin by charging God with wrongdoing" (Job 1:22). God doesn't cause human suffering. Suffering comes from the evil at work in this world. We live in an imperfect world where bad things happen even to good people. The goodness of God overcomes life's difficulties. "Surely goodness and mercy shall follow me all the days of my life" (Psalm 23:6 KJV). What a sure promise to those who honor the name of the Lord!

A distressed young woman came to our church one day and poured out her heart. The man she loved and hoped to spend the rest of her life with had abruptly moved out of town, got a new job, and ended their relationship.

She said, "I can't eat or sleep. I have no goals in life. I have a hard time concentrating on anything." Then she stopped, got a grip on herself, looked straight at me, and said, "Listen to me. I sound just like a sad country song!"

One night I preached at an inner-city church in Atlanta. The audience consisted mainly of homeless people who came to hear the Gospel and get a good meal. The church was a center for education and training so people could get on their feet and make it in the world. The pastor led the people in a triumphant confession:

"God is good!" he shouted.

The people responded, "All the time!"

"And all the time," the pastor shouted.

"God is good," came the refrain.

After they repeated this declaration three times, getting louder each time, the message was clear to everyone—God is good!

We misuse God's name when we blame Him for the bad things that happen in life. God's name is synonymous with His goodness. Whatever difficulties you may be facing, one fact remains: "God is good all the time. And all the time God is good!"

Charles Spurgeon once said, "When we bless God for mercies, we prolong them. When we bless Him for miseries, we usually end them."

Walk the Walk

We misuse God's name when we don't live up to our faith. Paul spoke of those who "claim to know God, but by their actions they deny him" (Titus 1:16). They talk the talk but don't walk the walk. Scholar William Barclay wrote: "The Christian dare not say, 'I care not what men say or think of me.' He must care, for his life is a testimony for or against his faith."

The word *sincerity* comes from Latin and means, "without wax." The Greek word means "sun-tested." The ancients made fine porcelain which was very expensive. Often when fired in the kiln, tiny cracks would form in the vessels. Dishonest merchants would fill the cracks with pearly-white wax to hide the cracks. A customer would not know the vessel was flawed unless he held the vessel up to the sun. The sun revealed the cracks. Honest dealers made their flawless products without wax.[11]

Sitting in a restaurant one Sunday with my family, a man I had never seen before walked over to our table. He shook my hand and said, "I've been watching you preach on your television program. I just wanted you to know that I appreciate your sincerity." Apparently, our sincerity comes through whether we realize it or not. People know when we're faking it and they know when our faith in Christ is real.

We misuse God's name when we violate oaths taken in His name. "When you make a vow to God, do not delay in fulfilling it. He has no pleasure in fools; fulfill your vow. It is better not to make a vow than to make one and not fulfill it" (Ecclesiastes 5:4-5). So, how can we honor the name of God?

Keep It Sacred

The name of God was so sacred to the ancient Hebrews that they would never speak it or write the full name. Instead, they abbreviated *Jehovah* with the letters

---

[11] Charles R. Swindoll, *The Quest for Character* (Multnomah, 1987), 67.

YWHW. That is how it appears in the original manuscripts of the Old Testament. The name of God was only spoken once a year by the High Priest on the Day of Atonement. This is one of the ways they were taught to treasure the sacred name of God. Jesus taught us to pray, "Our Father, who art in heaven, hallowed be thy name."

Gladys Aylward learned the power of God's name. As a missionary to China when World War 2 broke out, she was forced to leave when the Japanese invaded China. Yet, she could not bring herself to leave her work behind. So, with only one assistant, she led more than 100 orphans over the mountains toward Free China.

As she and the orphans traveled the treacherous journey all the way to Free China, fear gripped her heart. One night as the children slept under the open sky, she spent a sleepless night in despair. She felt they had no hope of reaching Free China.

The next morning, she gathered the kids together. "I'm sorry," she said. "I should have never taken you on this treacherous journey. We may not make it."

A young girl spoke up. "Miss Gladys, don't you remember the story about Moses and the Red Sea?" she asked. "Jehovah God brought them across safely."

"But I'm not Moses," Gladys replied.

"We know you aren't," the little girl said, "but Jehovah is still God."

Gladys and her orphans made it through to safety as a living testimony that Jehovah is still God.

Total Trust

The word *trust* best describes our relationship to God. The Hebrew concept of *trust* means to "roll the weight upon, rely upon, lean upon, and take refuge in the Lord." The psalmist wrote, "Some trust in chariots and some in horses, but we trust in the name of the Lord our God" (Psalm 20:7).

We trust only to the degree that we know someone. The same is true in our relationship with God. People don't trust God because they don't really know Him. We can trust His *wisdom* because He knows what is best for us. We can trust His *goodness* because He only desires what is best for us. And we can trust His *power* because He is able to do what is best for us. When you know God, you will trust Him.

Trust means, "Don't doubt in the dark what God has shown you in the light." Trust God when you're in the valley of defeat as much as you do when you stand on the mountain peak of victory. Anybody can trust God when everything is going the way they planned. But only a person of true faith can trust God in tough times. They know beyond a shadow of a doubt that Jehovah is the Promise Keeper.

The great industrialist Robert G. LeTourneau, manufacturer of earth-moving equipment, received a wartime order from the government to develop a machine to lift airplanes. No such machine had ever been conceived, much less built.

LeTourneau and his engineers went to work on the problem. They were baffled. Every think-tank meeting came up empty. Frustration set in. One Wednesday, as evening approached, the team was feverishly at work. LeTourneau, got up from the meeting and said, "Well, fellows, I'm leaving to go to prayer meeting at my church."

"Prayer meeting?" they said. "You can't do that. We've got a deadline to meet."

"But I've got a deadline with God," he responded.

He went to the prayer meeting. Forgetting his problem, he worshiped the Lord and got his mind off his issues as he prayed for others. On his way home, he reported that suddenly, the design of the machine appeared in his mind, complete with every detail. When LeTourneau got to the office the next morning, he called the design team together, gave them the plan, and they worked out all the details to build the machinery needed by the military.

Name Recognition

Jesus taught us to pray in His name. "You may ask for anything in my name and I will do it" (John 14:13). The content of our prayers must honor Jesus and conform to His will if we are to truly pray in His name. We can't just pray whatever we want and add the words "in Jesus' name" and think that's what prayer means. When we pray in the name of Jesus we pray according to His will. We pray, "Your kingdom come, your will be done."

We can also bless others in the name of the Lord. It is a powerful thing to bless someone in the name of the Lord. Jesus went so far as to say, "Bless those who curse you."

Let me share a funny family story with you. Our family was eating lunch one day. My daughter Charlsi was seven years old. She sneezed abruptly. I mean, she really sneezed. No one said anything. She looked around waiting for someone to say, "Bless you." But no one did. So, she said, "Bless me," and went on eating her lunch.

The Hebrew word *bless* is used 330 times in the Bible

and means "to kneel, to honor." The Greek word *eulogy* means "to speak well of and to bestow favor and honor on someone." Blessing means to praise God for who He is and for the blessings He gives us. When we bless others, we speak well of them, honor them, praise them, affirm them, and desire their highest good.

While the priests spoke the following blessing over the people of Israel, we can also speak this blessing over our family and friends: "The Lord bless you and keep you; the Lord make his face shine on you and be gracious to you; the Lord turn his face toward you and give you peace" (Numbers 6:24-26). God told Moses about the power of this blessing: "So they will put my name on the Israelites, and I will bless them" (v. 27). There's power in the blessing!

The blessing is always spoken. Remember, the word *blessing* means to honor or, literally, "to bow the knee." This refers to the act of showing respect and honor to an important person. Everyone needs praise. The greatest gift we can give another person is sincere praise which builds their confidence, self-esteem, and self-worth.

The name of Jesus brings hope. "For there is no other name under heaven given to mankind by which we must be saved" (Acts 4:12).

A man greeted me after a Sunday service. He said, "I've been attending your church for the last eight Sundays. During this time, I have accepted Christ and my life has been changed."

He went on to say, "Several months ago I came to Atlanta running away from my marriage, which was on the rocks. I came to Atlanta to leave my wife. Since Jesus Christ has become Lord of my life, I am a new person. I wanted to tell you good-bye today. I'm on my way back home to New York to my wife and family. Please pray that God will complete His work of healing in our home."

George Grenfell was a missionary to Africa many years ago who preached the gospel of Christ to remote tribes that were steeped in idolatry. He returned home for a short stay wondering if he had made any impact for Christ on the people.

Later, when he returned to Africa, his boat traveled down a tributary of the Congo River. He was met by a large group of men from a remote tribe. They began to sing powerfully, in their native tongue, "All hail the power of Jesus name, let angels prostrate fall; Bring forth the royal diadem and crown Him Lord of all. Bring forth the royal diadem and crown him, Lord of all!"

There's power in the name of the Lord. Let us use His name with wisdom, honor, and faith, knowing that His name brings hope and healing to the world.

5
GET SOME REST

"Remember the Sabbath day by keeping it holy."
Exodus 20:8-11

In April 1963, the nuclear submarine *Thresher* vanished about two hundred miles off the coast of New England. It had been undergoing deep submergence tests when radio contact was lost. Frantic attempts to contact, then to locate the crew were in vain. Apparently, the *Thresher* had gone deeper than it was pressurized to go. In one terrifying moment, the pressure on the outside became greater than the pressure within. Jets of ocean streams rushed in, and 129 American sailors were lost.

According to the American Institute of Stress, as many as 90 percent of visits to primary-care physicians are stress-related. Stress is a state of emotional, physical, and mental tension. Simply put, stress results from unrelieved tension. The word *stress* comes from a Latin word meaning "to draw tight or constrict." Stress increases our metabolism, pumping three to four times more blood to the muscles than normal. We experience a flight-or-fight response. Unfortunately, we often do neither. A surplus of adrenaline in the body causes emotional and physical problems.

We need enough stress to keep us motivated to achieve our goals. Stress serves as a warning system in the body alerting us to possible danger. If not handled properly, it becomes a toxin. Why are we so stressed out? Situational stress is work-related stress, personal problems, financial pressure, time demands, health issues, national and global adversities. Then there is relational stress of marital problems, family tension, work conflict, and arguments. We also experience spiritual stress from feelings of sin, guilt, and spiritual oppression. While stress management involves exercise, time management, rest, and relaxation, the greatest power we have is our relationship to God.

When we are stressed out, we feel worried, anxious, and uptight. Physically, we experience fatigue, sleep disturbances, ulcers, indigestion, eating disorders, and high blood pressure. Mentally, we become negative in our thinking, ineffective in our creativity and uncertain in our decisions. Relationally, we withdraw from others and often react with angry outbursts and frustration. Spiritually, we feel estranged from God, lose our sense of joy, and experience motivational loss in spiritual disciplines.

Stress serves as a warning system in the body, alerting us to possible danger. If not handled properly, it becomes a toxin. The answer to stress is to get some rest.

Sabbath Misconceptions

Our spiritual life can help us handle stress. The fourth commandment says: *Remember the Sabbath day by keeping it holy.* The Sabbath rest is a great cure for stress. Many people have missed the joy of the Sabbath by turning it into a religious rule. Jesus said, "The Sabbath was made for man, not man for the Sabbath" (Mark 2:27).

Keeping the Sabbath does not mean it's the only day for worship. "Therefore do not let anyone judge you by what you eat or drink, or with regard to a religious festival, a New Moon celebration or a Sabbath day. These are a shadow of the things that were to come; the reality, however, is found in Christ" (Colossians 2:16-17). Here's a similar passage: "One person considers one day more sacred than another; another considers every day alike. Each of them should be fully convinced in their own mind" (Romans 14:5).

God instructs us to work six days a week. That's not a legalist rule but a common-sense principle for a balanced life. It's sound advice not to work every day of the week. That's the main point. So, the commandment that tell us to rest first tells us to work! We need to work more than we rest or chill out. Six days of work for every one day of rest is a strategy for success. Sometimes we emphasize chilling out when we need to be working out. We need to balance our time between work, play, and worship.

Jesus broke traditions about the Sabbath. It was on the Sabbath when Jesus and His disciples picked grain from a field, healed a man with a shriveled hand in the synagogue, and healed a woman from a physical infirmity. In each case, He was criticized by religious leaders for violating the Sabbath. He confronted their religious rigidity. "Is it lawful to heal on the Sabbath? If any of you has a sheep and it falls into a pit on the Sabbath, will you not take hold of it and lift it out? Therefore, it is lawful to do good on the Sabbath. The Son of Man is Lord of the Sabbath."[12] He didn't break the Sabbath but rather their

---

[12] Matthew 12:1-14; Mark 2:27; Luke 13:10-17.

traditions about the Sabbath. He did that intentionally to show the difference between tradition and truth.

The Sabbath is a day of rest and relaxation. It's a day for fun and laughter. It's a day for recreation and leisure. It's a day to get together with God's people to worship, to hear the Word of God proclaimed, and to encourage others in their faith. Faithful church attendance is one of the most important spiritual habits that lead to a healthy life. Let us not "[give] up meeting together, as some are in the habit of doing, but [encourage] one another—and all the more as [we] see the Day [of Christ's return] approaching" (Hebrews 10:25). Going to church is one of the most important things families should do together to build their home on a foundation of faith.

It's a Celebration!

The Sabbath is God's gift to us. The Sabbath is more than a day of the week; it's an Old Testament type of Jesus, who gives us spiritual rest. Jesus is the Sabbath! God gave the Sabbath to remember His work of creation and redemption. Sabbath worship focuses first on creation. The Genesis account of creation reads, "Then God blessed the seventh day and made it holy, because on it he rested from all the work of creating that he had done" (Genesis 2:3). The word *rested* means God ceased from His work. Creation was complete. God rested not because He was tired but because He had finished the work and ceased from His labor of creation.

The themes of "creation" and "redemption" travel together in Scripture. The Creation account of the universe uses the language of God's plan of salvation. The Apostle John uses the language of Genesis to explain the coming of Jesus: "In the beginning was the Word, and the Word was with God, and the Word was God. He was with God in the beginning. Through him all things were made; without him nothing was made that has been made. In him was life, and that life was the light of all mankind" (John 1:1-3).

Just as God completed the work of creation, He has also completed the work of salvation. Jesus shouted triumphantly from the cross, "It is finished!" Now, by faith, we rest in the finished work of Christ who redeemed us from our sins. "Now we who have believed enter that rest" (Hebrews 4:3). The "rest" of which he speaks is the finished work of the cross. We don't labor for our salvation by good works. We rest in the finished work of Christ that gives us eternal life.

You can't earn forgiveness of sins and the promise of eternal life by doing good works. You must cease from your works and come to God by faith. Trust in what Jesus did for you on the Cross. It is in trusting, not trying, that we are saved. When Christians gather for worship on the Lord's Day, we are celebrating God's finished work of creation and redemption. Sunday is celebration day!

Break Time

I worked on a construction crew in downtown Atlanta the summer after my first year in college. The break truck came by promptly at 10 a.m. and 2 p.m. We were union workers, and those guys took their breaks religiously. As soon as the truck drove up, somebody yelled, "The break truck is here!" Instantly, everybody dropped their tools and headed to the truck for snacks. The Sabbath is God's break truck sent to us once a week to drop what we are doing and to stop working. God gave the Sabbath as a day of rest, recreation, and renewal. The first use of the word *Sabbath* is found in Exodus 16:23. After God provided manna and quail for the Israelites in the desert, He declared a holy Sabbath for them. They prepared all the food in advance for this special Sabbath day.

Workaholics hit a saturation point at work, after which they become less productive even though they keep working. It's called the law of diminishing returns. You keep working more but accomplishing less. Once a week God says, "It's break time!" Take a break and you'll lower your stress.

Keeping the Sabbath frees us from materialism. Prosperity is a great blessing, but it has its challenges. Thomas Carlyle, the Scottish essayist, said, "For every person who can handle prosperity there are a hundred who can handle adversity."

Money problems come in a lot of forms. "For the love of money is the root of all evil" (1 Timothy 6:10 KJV). Money isn't the root of all evil, but the love of money—the all-consuming desire for money, the worry about money, the measuring of life only by material standards—is the root of all kinds of evil.

Prosperity is a double-edged sword. We can use our wealth for noble purposes. We can also fall asleep in the lap of luxury. Jesus cautioned, "Watch out! Be on your guard against all kinds of greed; a man's life does not consist in an abundance of possessions" (Luke 12:15).

When we keep the Sabbath, we stop pursuing the material so we can pursue the spiritual. "Set your hearts on things above" (Colossians 3:1). Jesus tells us to seek first the kingdom of God and all these other things will be given to us (Matthew 6:33). Truett Cathy, founder of Chick-fil-A, tried it and succeeded. His stores have remained closed on Sunday since he founded the business. However, the business thrives under the blessings of God. The psalmist David prayed, "You, God, are my God, earnestly I seek you" (Psalm 63:1). That is the spirit of the Sabbath.

Get Connected

The Sabbath has always been a day for worship. Christianity is community. We are the family of God and families love getting together. Powerful things happen when God's people come together. Jesus promised, "Where two or three gather in my name, there am I with them" (Matthew 18:20).

The word *church* comes from a Greek word that means a "public assembly." The church is the spiritual body of Christ made up of every person who confesses Jesus Christ as Lord. God gave us the church as our spiritual family. The church is the place where faith is nurtured, character is molded, and talents are used to serve others.

You might find this research interesting: Active church members have a 60 percent less chance of a heart attack. Active church members live an average of 5.7 years longer. Active church members who see God as their life partner have fewer colds, headaches, and ulcers. The National Institute of Health once showed five ways to help fight heart disease. The leading one was weekly church attendance. I once read a report by a life insurance company that showed the single most important variable in the health promoting lifestyles was religious affiliation.

When Jesus used the word *church*, He meant the gathering of His followers. Every Christian makes up the church. The church is people, but the people gather in a place. "When the day of Pentecost came, they were all together in one place" (Acts 2:1). Smart phones and computers enable us to go to church when we travel for business or vacation or otherwise are unable to attend in person. While technology is a great tool, it can never fully replace the power of personal relationships when we get together to worship the Lord and to encourage each other. A computer screen is one-dimensional; but life is 3-D! By going to church, you will receive incredible personal benefits and you will benefit others. The church needs you, and you need the church!

Since the time of Moses, Jewish people have kept the Sabbath. Early Christians began worshiping on the first day of the week in celebration of Christ's resurrection, which occurred on the first day of the week (1 Corinthians 16:2). During the early days of the newborn church, Jewish Christians continued to observe the Sabbath and worshiped in the synagogues. Later, Sunday took on special significance as the Christian Sabbath. Sunday will always be a special day for the people of God. On Sunday, the followers of Jesus went in sorrow to His tomb but left ecstatic with joy because the grave was empty.

When Christians worship on Sunday, we are celebrating new life. "Why do you look for the living among the dead? He is not here; he has risen!" (Luke 24:5-6). Sunday is a day of hope, new beginnings, and a fresh start. As the first day of the week, Sunday sets the tone for the rest of the week, giving us a new outlook and preparing us to live for the glory of God.

Running on Empty

Recently, our nation experienced a gas shortage because of a cyberattack on an oil pipeline. Gas stations all along the east coast ran completely out of gas. People panicked when they had no gas for their cars. We can't function without fuel. Many of our health problems are due to stress because we've run out of the energy and enthusiasm we need to cope with life.

I'm sure you've heard the adage, "That got my goat." Well, in ancient times people who raised racing horses would put a goat in the stall with the horses, especially the day before the race. The goat's quiet, calm demeanor would keep the horse calm. Rival owners sometimes stole another man's goat out of the stall the night before the race so the horse would be high-strung and not run as well. Hence the phrase, "That got my goat." So, don't let all the stress get your goat!

One of my favorite psalms is Psalm 84. The psalmist writes, "Blessed are those whose strength is in you, whose hearts are set on pilgrimage. As they pass through the Valley of Baca, they make it a place of springs; the autumn rains also cover it with pools. They go from strength to strength" (vv. 5-7).

The Hebrew word *Baca* means "weeping, sorrow, bitterness." As we pass through the valley of hardship and difficulty, weeping and bitterness, we can turn it into a place of springs and pools of refreshing water. What a picture of what God does for us when we worship Him and enter His presence! The word *pools* in Hebrew means "blessings." Everyone needs a Sabbath rest for stressful living. Stop frequently at God's oasis and receive fresh strength. You, too, can go from strength unto strength.

Urgent or Important?

If you're like me, I'm sure you get caught up in the rat race from time to time. (Just remember, only the rats win!) Misplaced priorities. Hectic schedules. Anxious thoughts. Tense relationships. You feel like you're doing what you're supposed to do but not what you want to do. You're driven by the tyranny of the urgent. You feel like you're getting pulled in a hundred directions.

We can identify with the guy who bought a Vespa scooter to drive to work. One morning he pulled up to a traffic light next to a new BMW. He liked it so much that the driver opened his door so the man could get a look inside. As the Vespa driver was leaning over, looking in the car, the light turned green. The driver slammed the door and sped away.

Suddenly, he saw the Vespa catching up to him and then pass him. Ahead, the Vespa stopped on a dime, whirled around, and came right back toward the BMW. Then it crashed in the middle of the street.

The BMW pulled his car over, pulled down the window and asked, "Man, are you OK?"

The Vespa driver said, "I think so."

"Is there anything I can do for you?" the BMW driver asked.

"Yes," he replied. "You can open your car door and let go of my suspenders!"

That's life in the fast lane. The Sabbath gives us a special time to stop the hustle and bustle and enter the secret place of the Lord's presence where He leads you beside still waters and restores your soul.

Learn to distinguish the urgent from the important. The urgent drives us relentlessly. The urgent disrupts our lives with constant demands of *do it now*. Don't allow your schedule to control you; you need to take control of your schedule. Don't try to meet all the urgent demands that come up. Focus on the important and let the urgent take care of itself. Learn to say no to things that are not priorities to you.

Jesus knew the difference between the important and the urgent. He said "he can only do what he sees his Father doing" (John 5:19). He was in perfect control of His time and faced every challenge with utmost confidence. He was never driven; He was only led by God's agenda for His life. He once told His family and His disciples, "My time is not yet here; for you any time will do" (7:6). Are you in control of your life or are you driven by the tyranny of the urgent? It's time to take charge of your schedule.

Get Your Rest

The Sabbath is more than a day of the week. The Sabbath is a Person. Jesus said, "Come to me, all you who are weary and burdened, and I will give you rest. Take my yoke upon you and learn from me, for I am gentle and humble in heart, and you will find rest for your souls" (Matthew 11:28-29).

He declared Himself to be the Sabbath rest for those who labor trying to find rest for their soul. The spiritual Sabbath begins when you trust Jesus as your Lord and Savior. "We who have believed enter that rest" (Hebrew 4:3). Don't try to earn God's love by doing good works. Accept His love by faith. Eternal life is a gift from God, not a work we do. Remember, "There remains, then, a Sabbath-rest for the people of God; for anyone who enters God's rest also rests from their works, just as God did from his" (Hebrews 4:9-10).

Here's a fascinating interpretation of Psalm 23 that captures the meaning of the Sabbath rest for the stress of life:

The Lord is my pacesetter, I shall not rush.

He makes me stop and rest for quiet intervals,

He provides me with images of stillness which deepen my serenity.

He leads me in ways of efficiency through calmness of mind,

And His guidance is peace.

Even though I have a great many things to accomplish each day,

I will not fret, for His presence is here.

His timelessness, His all importance will keep me in balance.

He prepares refreshment and renewal during my activity.

By anointing my mind with oils of tranquility,

My cup of joyous energy overflows.

Surely harmony and effectiveness shall be the fruits of my hours.

For I shall walk in the pace of the Lord,

And dwell in His house forever.

6
HEALTHY HOMES

"Honor your father and your mother, so that you may live long in the land the Lord your God is giving you."
Exodus 20:12

A famous comedian said, "Happiness is having a large, loving close-knit family—in another city." Family living can be challenging, especially for parents. Everything you try as a parent is trial and error. When I made mistakes, I told my kids, "Hey, give me a break! I've never been a parent before."

I once read that raising small children is about as easy as nailing a poached egg to a tree. Family living is the greatest blessing in life, yet it can be the most challenging experience of life. Every family would like to live stress-free. Family stress is defined as real or imagined demands on a family versus the ability to meet those demands. Such demands are work, finances, schedule, illness, relocation, death, and life changes.

Here are some family facts about Americans: People are waiting longer to get married. On average, men are 29 and women are 27. Couples are having less children with only an average of 1.9 children per family (versus

3.7 children in 1960). When the birthrate is lower than 2.1 children per home, our population diminishes. More children are being born to single mothers than ever before. Traditional families with a father, mother, and their children make up only 16 percent of homes (versus 37 percent in 1960). The national average length of marriage is 8.2 years.

Here are some funny quotes about family:

"A family is a social unit where the father is concerned with parking space, the children with outer space, and the mother with closet space."

"Family is like fudge—mostly sweet with a few nuts."

"If you don't believe in ghosts, you've probably never been to a family reunion."

"Insanity is hereditary—you can get it from your children!"

"What do grandparents and grandkids have in common? The same enemy!"

The fifth commandment speaks to family living: *Honor your father and your mother, so that you may live long in the land the Lord your God is giving you.* While this commandment addresses children, it also speaks to parents. Children are commanded to honor and obey their parents. Parents are called to create a healthy climate in the home so children can grow in the virtues of honor and obedience.

Honor and Obey

What is honor and obedience, and why are they so important in life that we need to learn these values as children? Honor and obedience to God's authority and to human authority provide the basis for a lawful society. It's no coincidence that America's social problems parallel the breakdown of the family. As the family goes, so goes the nation. Children who learn to honor their parents also show respect for God and for others in authority. The word *honor* means "to prize others highly, to demonstrate care and affection, and to show respect and reverence."

Can children be expected to cultivate such virtues on their own? How can innocent children who face instability, insensitivity, negligence, or abuse learn to honor their parents? Children simply respond to what parents do and say. Parents must first honor and value their children as God's gift to them in order for children to learn honor and obedience.

One father said he changed his prayer from, "Lord, change my children," to "Lord, change my children's father."

While we may not want to admit it, our children are mirrors reflecting our attitudes and actions. Parents who honor their children by caring for them raise children who honor and obey them. We reap what we sow in our homes.

Healthy families are based on climate control. Paul connected the command to children with the command to parents. "Children obey your parents in the Lord," is followed by, "Fathers do not exasperate your children; instead, bring them up in the training and instruction of the Lord" (Ephesians 6:1-4). We need to change the thermostat in homes to the comfortable setting of faith, hope, and love. That's the climate of a healthy home.

Trust or Mistrust

Social psychologist Eric Erickson observed that the first stage of personality development in a child's life is learning to trust. He called the first stage of life a crisis point of "trust versus mistrust." By age two, children either trust people because they feel safe, or they develop a sense of mistrust with anxiety about the world. Trust is the foundation of all healthy relationships, including our relationship with God. "Trust in the Lord with all your heart" is only possible because God loves us and cares for us (Proverbs 3:5).

Healthy children feel secure, loved, accepted, and valued. Love is the antidote to fear. We are born with only two fears: the fear of falling and the fear of loud noises. All other fears are learned. Little children develop imaginary fears like fear of the dark or fear of monsters lurking in the bedroom closet.

The burst of thunder sent a terrified three-year old running from her bed into her parent's bedroom. "Mommy, I'm scared," she said. "I want to get in bed with you and Daddy."

Her mother, half-awake, replied, "It's okay, sweetheart. Go back to bed. There's no reason to be afraid. God is in your room with you."

Unconvinced, she climbed into the bed and snuggled safely between her parents and said, "Mommy, you go in there and sleep with God. I'm sleeping in here with Daddy!"

Teenagers face social fears of acceptance or rejection, success or failure, inclusion or exclusion. Teens are easily embarrassed in front of their peers. I didn't like the car my dad drove when I was in high school. One morning when he drove me to school, I asked him to stop at the curb and let me out, so no one saw the car. The car was fine, but I didn't think it looked cool enough. I was overly concerned about my friends and what they would think. Teens exaggerate their pressures, especially parental pressures. Even too much praise from parents can be mistaken as a demand for perfection. Teens and college students also worry about world events and global concerns. Perhaps now more than ever, kids need a safe, secure home so they can grow in confidence in God and in themselves. Cultivating the climate of safety and security at home is the starting point for raising healthy kids.

Time Together

Kids need time with their parents. There's no substitute for spending time with your children. You, as a parent, will not only teach them, but they'll also teach you a few things. When my daughter Charlsi was five, I learned a new way of looking at insomnia. I went to bed late one night. As I reached the top of the stairs, my eyes caught a glimpse of her lying upside down on the bed with her feet facing the headboard. Her head was resting in the palms of her hands. Thinking something might be wrong with her, I went into her room.

"Charlsi, are you okay?" I asked.

She said, "Dad, I can't get my head to go to sleep."

Some reports show that fewer than 25 percent of young boys and girls experience an average of at least one hour a day of individual contact with their fathers. The average daily amount of personal time fathers spend with their children is less than 30 minutes. In the beautiful Yiddish song "My Angel," written in 1887, a father sings to his son as he sleeps:

I have a son, a little son, a boy completely fine.
Whenever I see him, it seems to me that all the world is mine.
But seldom, seldom do I see my child awake and bright.
I only see him when he sleeps; I'm only home at night.
It's early when I leave for work; when I return, it's late.
Unknown to me is my own flesh, unknown is my child's face.
When I come home so wearily in the darkness after day,
My pale wife exclaims to me: "You should have seen our child play."
I stand beside his little bed; I look and try to hear.
In his dream he moves his lips: "Why isn't Papa here?"

What greater experience can a child have than to be held safely in their parents' arms and be told, "I love you"? And what a blessing for parents! One-third of the five million touch receptors in the human body are centered in the hands. A UCLA study showed that every person needs eight to ten meaningful touches a day to maintain emotional and physical health. Dr. Dolores Krieger, professor of nursing at New York University, has made numerous studies on the physical benefits from the laying on of hands. Inside our bodies is hemoglobin, the pigment of the red blood cells, which carries oxygen to other tissues. Dr. Krieger has found repeatedly that hemoglobin levels in our bloodstream rise during the act of the laying on of hands in both the giver and the recipient. Increased levels of hemoglobin provide more oxygen to body tissues, which aids in the regeneration process when someone is ill.[13]

---

[13] John Trent and Gary Smalley, *The Blessing* (Nashville: Thomas Nelson, 1986), 39-42.

Jesus knew the power of touch. He touched a leper and cleansed him. He touched Peter's mother-in-law and relieved her from fever. He touched a blind man and made him see. He touched children as He blessed them. His ministry was not in word only but in the power of His healing touch. Most importantly, "He took the children in his arms, put his hands on them and blessed them" (Mark 10:15).

A freelance writer from the *New York Times* interviewed Marilyn Monroe. He knew that Marilyn had been shuffled from foster home to foster home when she was a young child. The reporter asked her, "Did you ever feel loved by any of the foster families with whom you lived?"

"Once," Marilyn replied, "when I was about seven or eight. The woman I was living with was putting on make-up, and I was watching her. She was in a happy mood, so she reached over and patted my cheeks with her rouge puff. . . . For that moment, I felt loved by her." The simple act of touching showered blessings of love on a little girl starved for affection.

Tell Them

Washington Irving was right when he said, "The tongue is the only tool that grows sharper with constant use." Words can bless or curse, heal or wound, build up or tear down. Healthy families practice healthy communication.

Words are very powerful. Here's a crash course on communication: "Do not let any unwholesome talk come out of your mouths, but only what is helpful for building others up according to their needs, that it may benefit those who listen" (Ephesians 4:29). The word *benefit* means "to bestow a blessing on others or to speak well of them."

Honor starts with the way we speak to each other at home. The word *honor* literally means "to bow the knee," referring to the act of showing awe and reverence to an important person. Everyone needs praise. The greatest gift parents can give their children, besides their faith in God, is the gift of self-esteem. When kids feel good about themselves, they can face life with confidence and adequacy.

James Taylor sings, "Shower the people you love with love." Kids don't deal well with silence. A little girl was going to summer camp for the first time. Her older brother, Jimmy, was going to camp with her. Her parents were concerned that she would get homesick. When they picked the kids up at the end of the camp to go home, they asked if she got homesick.

"Sometimes I did," she replied, "but I would just go over to Jimmy's cabin, and he would yell, 'GET OUT OF HERE!' and then I'd feel okay again."

Parents need to tell their children two powerful affirmations to prepare them to face life with confidence:

We love you no matter what.
We believe in you no matter what.

Winston Churchill said, "We all are worms, but I do believe I am a glowworm." The psalmist reminds us, "I praise you because I am fearfully and wonderfully made; your works are wonderful, I know that full well" (Psalm 139:14). Children need to be reminded often, through encouraging words, that they are fearfully and wonderfully made. Or, in the words of Churchill, they are glowworms.

While positive speaking is vital to healthy communication, so is attentive listening. Parents need to listen to their kids. We are so focused on telling them what to do that we fail to listen to them. Do we really listen to our kids? Are we aware of the issues they're dealing with? Kids, especially teenagers, deal with so many personal, social, and global concerns. Children are dealing with more anxiety and depression than ever before. Social media has some positive benefits, but it also opens the door to bullying, self-preoccupation about one's appearance, and social rejection.

Parents need to know about their kids and that comes from listening to them. *What do they dream about? What would they like to be when they grow up? What subjects do they most enjoy the most and the ones they least enjoy? Do they have a boyfriend or girlfriend? What do they believe about God? What's going on with them spiritually? Who's their best friend?*

Kids love to talk, and if we as parents ask them questions, they will tell us what's going on. We want our kids to tell us their greatest dreams and deepest worries. Listening is love in action.

Bring Them Up

The early American painter Benjamin West tells how he became an artist. One day his mother went to run some errands and left him in charge of his little sister, Sally. While she was gone, he discovered some bottles of colored ink and decided to paint Sally's portrait. When he finished the painting, he realized he had made a horrendous mess in the process. He had permanently stained his clothes and the furniture where he was drawing.

When his mother came home and saw the mess, she was shocked initially but said nothing. She then picked up the piece of paper and looked with great interest at the drawing. She said, "Benjamin, this is a wonderful picture of your sister." She picked him up and kissed him. Benjamin West used to say, "My mother's kiss made me a painter."

Good parents do everything with a spirit of affirmation. We seek to build up and never put down our children. I played basketball in high school. One very good player from another school had a father who was overbearing. He would put him on restriction as punishment if he missed a free throw in a game. God's Word teaches us as parents to affirm our children so that they succeed in life. Affirmation leads to achievement. "Fathers, do not exasperate your children; instead, bring them up in the training and instruction of the Lord" (Ephesians 6:4).

The word *exasperate* means to arouse anger, to irritate, or to frustrate. The Apostle Paul also wrote to parents, "Do not embitter your children or they will become discouraged" (Colossians 3:21). We exasperate and embitter our children by extreme perfectionism, pressure to perform, and excessive punishment. The secret to raising healthy and happy kids is "to bring them up in the training and instruction of the Lord." Bring them up and never put them down. When parents believe in their kids, they will believe in themselves and reach their highest potential. If you, as a parent, bring them up, no one will be able to put them down!

I read that our praises should outweigh our corrections three to one for kids to be psychologically healthy. When Paul tells parents to bring their children up in the training and instruction of the Lord, he puts the emphasis on *bring them up*. That stands in sharp contrast to putting them down.

The home is the primary place for the training and instruction of the Lord. The greatest university in the world is the Christian home. The greatest professor is a loving parent. Our basic training for life comes from the home. Churches and schools can only support what happens at home.

A senator was talking to a group of concerned parents about prayer in public schools at a public forum. He asked, "How many of you support prayer in public schools?" All the parents raised their hands in the affirmative.

"Now, let me ask you," he continued, "do you pray with your kids before you send them to school?"

Children learn about God from their parents. They learn to distinguish right from wrong at home. They develop a healthy conscience at home and form their core values for life. The greatest ministry in the world is parents who bring their children up in the training and instruction of the Lord.

Church in Your House

My mother spoke at our church one Mother's Day. Her message was titled, "The Church That Meets in Your House." It was taken from Paul's commendation to a married couple who were leaders in the church, Aquilla and Priscilla. Paul gave a shout-out to "the church that meets at their house" (1 Corinthians 16:19). My mother's message made an impression on me. The home is the center of our spiritual development.

Faith in God starts at home. "Day after day, in the Temple courts and from house to house, they never stopped teaching and proclaiming . . . that Jesus is the Messiah" (Acts 5:42). Keep the faith in private devotions and public worship. Jesus went to church at the synagogue every Sabbath. He also went to solitary places where He prayed. Share family devotions and take your family to church, and your family will be healthy.

I listened to an archbishop in New York say people must practice their faith to keep their faith. He said the global pandemic caused people to get out of the habit of going to church, which is a good habit. Let us "not [give] up meeting together, as some are in the habit of doing, but let us [encourage] one another—and all the more as you see the Day approaching" (Hebrews 10:25).

Keep the faith in good times and bad times. *Be grateful to God in the good times.* "When you have eaten and are satisfied, praise the Lord your God for the good land he has given you. Be careful that you do not forget the Lord your God . . . for it is he who gives you the ability to produce wealth, and so confirms his covenant" (Deuteronomy 8:10-11, 18).

Be faithful in the bad times. Job experienced hard times, but he kept the faith. He had rebellious children, but he prayed regularly for them (Job 1:5). He suffered health and financial problems and had a strained marriage, but he kept the faith. At the pinnacle of Job's suffering, he declared, "Though he slay me, yet will I hope in him. I will surely defend my ways to his face" (13:15). The family was blessed because of his faith. "The Lord restored his fortunes and gave him twice as much as he had before. . . . The Lord blessed the latter part of Job's life more than the former part" (42:10, 12).

Some of my fondest childhood memories are the times when we had family devotions. My father read one chapter from the Bible to us, usually after dinner. He especially liked Proverbs and the Book of James. I once asked him why he always read to us from these books. He replied, "Because they're full of down-to-earth wisdom. And you kids need it."

Faith is caught as well as taught. Children do what they see us doing, and they say what they hear us say. They are watching us all the time, and they are learning when we don't realize it. The following anonymous poem reminds us that our kids are watching us all the time.

When you thought I wasn't looking, I saw you hang my first painting on the refrigerator, and I wanted to paint another one.

When you thought I wasn't looking, I saw you feed a stray cat, and I thought it was good to be kind to animals.

When you thought I wasn't looking, I saw you make my favorite cake just for me, and I knew that little things are special things.

When you thought I wasn't looking, I heard you say a prayer, and I believed there is a God I could always talk to.

When you thought I wasn't looking, I felt you kiss me goodnight, and I felt loved.

When you thought I wasn't looking, I saw tears come from your eyes, and I learned that sometimes things hurt, but it's all right to cry.

When you thought I wasn't looking, I saw you cared, and I wanted to be everything that I could be.

When you thought I wasn't looking, I looked . . .
and wanted to say thanks for all the things I saw
when you thought I wasn't looking.

Let's be on the lookout for our kids to do what's right, then pour on the praise. Encouraging good behavior is a more effective way of teaching than correcting bad behavior. It's unhealthy for parents to only give their kids attention when they mess up. That's parenting from behind. Get out in front of your children and lead them by praising the good things they do, and you won't have to correct them as much. While correction is important for their growth, encouragement is more important. So, watch carefully when they share their toys, treat someone kindly, apologize without having to be told to do it, or get their homework done on their own—then pour on the praise.

One of the more obscure exhibitions in the Smithsonian Institute displays the personal articles found on Abraham Lincoln the night he was assassinated. They include a small handkerchief embroidered A. *Lincoln*, a country boy's pen knife, an eyeglass case repaired with cotton string, a Confederate $5 bill, and a worn-out newspaper clipping praising his accomplishments as President. It begins with the words, "Abe Lincoln is one of the greatest statesmen of all time."

Why would he keep an article like that on his person? Although Lincoln is considered one of America's greatest Presidents, he faced a lot of opposition. He was not very popular and faced bitter criticism at times. So, he carried something for encouragement and affirmation. The article reminded him that someone believed in him; this, in turn, helped him to believe in himself.

Let's teach our children to believe in God and to believe in themselves. When we do, they will grow up to face life with confidence and courage, and they will be empowered to make a difference in the world for the glory of God.

7
MURDER MYSTERY

"You shall not murder."

Exodus 20:13

I grew up in the city of Atlanta. Over the years, I have watched the city grow and flourish. Atlanta is a beautiful city. But, like many urban centers, its beauty lies obscured by a dark cloud of violence. What has happened to America the Beautiful? Violent crimes have surged recently in the major cities of America with social unrest, lawlessness, and efforts to defund police. Some politicians even advocate getting rid of law enforcement and replacing it with social workers.

The Bible is clear that laws exist for the lawbreaker, not for the law-abiding. "We also know that the law is made not for the righteous but for lawbreakers and rebels, the ungodly and sinful, the unholy and irreligious" (1 Timothy 1:9). Only the lawless want to get rid of laws and law enforcement.

Today, violent crime and murders are on a sharp rise in our nation. Jesus foretold the increased violence in the last days. "Just as it was in the days of Noah, so also will it be in the days of the Son of Man" (Luke 17:26). What was it like in Noah's day before the Flood? According to Genesis 6, "The earth was corrupt in God's sight and full of violence. Every inclination of men's hearts was only on evil continually. God saw how all the people had corrupted their ways. The Lord was grieved that he had made man on the earth and his heart was filled with pain. The Lord said, 'My Spirit will not always strive with man'" (see vv. 3-12).

The sixth commandment addresses the violence in our world—*You shall not murder.*

The word *kill* in Hebrew means "to commit murder." Some make the mistake of thinking the commandment forbids someone protecting himself or his family or that it prevents soldiers from fighting in combat, but it doesn't. God is speaking specifically about murder. Others think it forbids capital punishment, but it doesn't. The Bible provides grounds for capital punishment in cases of premeditated murder. "Whoever sheds man's blood, by man his blood shall be shed; for in the image of God He made man" (Genesis 9:6 NKJV). However, the administration of justice must be balanced with mercy. God spared Cain when he murdered his brother Abel, because his was a crime of passion. Capital punishment should be reserved for the most heinous crimes of premediated murder.

Some people conscientiously object to military service on the grounds of this commandment. This commandment does not forbid war. "War is hell," said General George Patton during World War II. Sadly, war is necessary for the defense of freedom and the protection of nations against aggression, invasion, and destruction. The nation of Israel is threatened by Islamic nations that openly call for their annihilation. One of the most important things America does is stand with Israel in the defense of their enemies. God blesses our nation because we support Israel. God used war to judge the wickedness of the Amorites (Genesis 15:16).

Historians view President Abraham Lincoln's second inaugural address to be his greatest speech ever. Given at the height of the Civil War, Lincoln said God chose "this mighty scourge of war" to punish both "the North and South" for the "American sin" and "offence" of slavery. He said God's judgments are true and righteous, quoting Psalm 19. He mentioned God fourteen times, prayer six times, the Bible specifically by name, cited several specific verses of Scripture, and claimed God hears and answers prayer and provides divine guidance for people who trust Him.

While war is terrible, the consequences of not fighting a war to defeat dictators, terrorist regimes, and totalitarian governments that want to rule the world would be far worse than the casualties of war. God has ordained that the history of this world will end with a final war called the Battle of Armageddon (Revelation 16:16). Then Jesus will return as King of kings to defeat the powers of darkness and establish the kingdom of God. The apostle saw a vision of Christ's return: "The armies of heaven were following him, riding on white horses and dressed in fine linen, white and clean. Coming out of his mouth is a sharp sword with which to strike down the nations. 'He will rule them with an iron scepter.' He treads the winepress of the fury of the wrath of God Almighty. On his robe and on his thigh he has this name written: 'KING OF KINGS AND LORD OF LORDS'" (19:14-16).

Freedom is never free and must, at times, be defended even at the terrible expense of war. "You shall not murder," does not refer to a just war for the defense of freedom and protection against tyranny. Our nation's freedom from British rule came at the cost of the War of Independence.

Beneath the Surface

Murder is the act, so what is the underlying cause? Lurking beneath the surface is deep-seated anger, rage, and hatred. When Jesus taught on this commandment, he dug beneath the surface of the act of murder to expose the anger behind the act:

> You have heard that it was said to the people long ago, "You shall not murder, and anyone who murders will be subject to judgment." But I tell you that anyone who is angry with a brother or sister will be subject to judgment. . . . Again, anyone who says to a brother or sister, "Raca," is answerable to the court. And, anyone who says, "You fool!" will be in danger of the fire of hell. Therefore, if you are offering your gift at the altar and there remember that your brother has something against you, leave your gift there in front of the altar. First go and be reconciled to them; then come and offer your gift (Matthew 5:21-24).

Violence stems from deep-seated anger, rage, and malice. Was Jesus saying anger or anger without a just cause is the same as murder? Absolutely not! Such a notion is utter foolishness. Would you rather someone *think* about stealing from you or steal a prized possession? Or, even more preposterous, would you prefer someone to get angry with you, or to take your life? Jesus was not saying anger is the same sin as murder. He was teaching that acts of violence begin in the heart.

The first murder in history reveals the underlying cause of anger:

> The Lord looked with favor on Abel and his offering, but on Cain and his offering he did not look with favor. So, Cain was very angry, and his face was downcast. Then the Lord said to Cain, "Why are you angry? Why is your face downcast? If you do what is right, will you not be accepted? But if you do not do what is right, sin is crouching at your door; it desires to have you, but you must rule over it" (Genesis 4:4-7).

When Cain failed to rule over his rage, he killed his brother. His anger was also fueled by his jealousy of Abel, whose offering was accepted by God while Cain's was rejected because he disobeyed God.

Violence is fueled by anger and jealousy in personal relationships, people groups, and entire nations. Violence is even rooted in generations of bitterness of one group of people toward another. Just as Edom "harbored an ancient hostility" (Ezekiel 35:5), some groups harbor bitterness over sins committed many generations ago of which none of us are responsible for today. Since they don't let it go, their anger festers into bitterness and resentment which, in turn, fuels violent words and acts.

People can be killed in other ways than by the act of murder. They can be killed verbally, emotionally, and psychologically. Love can be killed. Self-confidence can be killed. Innocence can be killed. Human potential can be killed. The destructive force of unbridled anger expressed through criticism, hatred, racism, bullying, and abuse (verbal, emotional and physical) kills. That is what

Jesus was talking about when He exposed the underlying cause of anger and rage that lurks beneath the surface.

Anger Analysis

Jesus said, "Anyone who is angry with his brother or sister will be subject to judgment" (Matthew 5:22). The King James Version adds, "angry with his brother without a cause," because it best expresses what Jesus meant. Did Jesus mean we will face judgment just because we get angry? Not at all. He was speaking of anger expressed inappropriately and anger that is not justified. We all get angry. Anger is an emotion, not a sin. Even God gets angry. There are 455 Old Testament references to anger, and 375 of them refer to God's anger. We also learn "[Jesus] looked around at them in anger" (Mark 3:5). He was angry with hypocritical religious leaders who judged others but never took a good look at themselves. If Jesus can get angry, so can we.

While the feeling of anger isn't sinful, if left unchecked or unresolved it can lead us into sin. "In your anger do not sin" (Ephesians 4:26). Unresolved anger can turn into rage, resentment, and bitterness. When we forgive others, we are free from anger. An exhibit was once presented at New York's Whitney Museum that devoted one entire section to "women's rage." Forgiveness is a more excellent way to live. Let's walk in the footsteps of Jesus who prayed for his executioners from the Cross, "Father, forgive them" (Luke 23:34). We live free only when we forgive.

Anger gets in the way of our spiritual growth. "Do not let the sun go down while you are still angry" (v. 26). Studies have linked anger to high-blood pressure, depression, psychological disturbances, and violence. "An angry person stirs up conflict, and a hot-tempered person commits many sins" (Proverbs 29:22). King David said, "Refrain from anger and turn from wrath . . . it leads only to evil" (Psalm 37:8).

The Apostle James wrote, "Everyone should be quick to listen, slow to speak and slow to become angry, because human anger does not produce the righteousness that God desires" (James 1:19-20). Spiritual growth is linked to the way we handle anger. As we yield our lives to Jesus as Lord, we can get anger under control and express it in a way that honors God and never hurts others.

Anger Sources

Anger stems from several sources. Anger can come from our *rebellion toward God*. Saul of Tarsus, a self-righteous Pharisee, "[breathed] out murderous threats against the [church]" (Acts 9:1). Finally, he encountered Jesus in a vision on the Damascus Road and repented of his sin. He called himself "the worst of sinners" (1 Timothy 1:15), because he blasphemed God and tried to the destroy the church. The anointing of the Holy Spirit on his life curbed his anger. He went on to build the Christian church he once tried to destroy, and he preached the gospel of Christ he once tried to silence. No wonder he said, "If anyone is in Christ, he is a new creation" (2 Corinthians 5:17 NKJV). Paul was transformed by God's amazing grace from an angry man to an anointed minister!

Persistent anger comes from *emotional immaturity*. Immaturity means we're frustrated because we cannot get what we want when we want it. So, we throw a temper tantrum. Some people never grow out of throwing temper tantrums. The answer to immaturity is, "Stop [acting] like children" (1 Corinthians 14:20).

Anger also stems from *jealousy*. King Saul was jealous of David. David was young, handsome, famous, and loved by everyone. He was a champion who killed the giant Goliath. His exploits were the subject of pop songs. Saul couldn't stomach the thought of God choosing David to be the next king of Israel. Saul wanted his son Jonathan to be the heir apparent to the throne of Israel. Interestingly, Jonathan loved David and protected him from his father. They shared a covenant of friendship. King Saul tried repeatedly to have David killed by his soldiers, but David escaped the attempts every time. God protected David. King Saul was tormented for years by his own jealousy and anger. In the end he destroyed himself and fell on his sword in battle.

The psalmist Asaph confessed his jealousy over the rich and successful: "Surely God is good to Israel, to those who are pure in heart. But as for me, my feet had almost slipped; I had nearly lost my foothold. For I envied the arrogant when I saw the prosperity of the wicked" (Psalm 73:1-3).

Asaph got angry because he was faithful to God, yet the unfaithful seemed to live a better life than him. His jealousy over their prosperity enraged him. He became angry toward God and nearly lost his faith over it. However, he let his anger go and regained his perspective. "When I tried to understand all this, it troubled me deeply till I entered the sanctuary of God; then I understood their final destiny. Surely you place them on slippery ground; you cast them down to ruin" (vv. 16-18).

Finally, he got free from anger as he worshiped in the sanctuary of God. "But as for me, it is good to be near God. I have made the Sovereign Lord my refuge; I will tell of all your deeds" (v. 28).

Anger also stems from high levels of *stress and pressure*. A test that measures chronic hostility was developed by Dr. Redford Williams and Virginia Williams for their book, *Anger Kills*. Research shows those who suffer from chronic hostility may be at risk of heart disease.

Finally, anger stems from *unfinished business of the past*. The number-one type of unfinished business is resentment. Some people struggle to get past hurt, trauma, injustice, and abuse. Our mental health requires us to settle the unfinished business of the past so we can be alive to the present. "See to it that no one falls short of the grace of God and that no bitter root grows up to cause trouble and defile many" (Hebrews 12:15). Take out your emotional trash every night and, "Do not let the sun go down while you are still angry" (Ephesians 4:26). Don't let the pain of the past rob you of the pleasure of the present.

How can we deal with anger? Here are some strategies not to use when managing anger:

Don't disguise your anger. You don't need to repress your anger and opt for peace. Don't play the role of the martyr and allow people to mistreat you. Turning the other cheek doesn't mean to take abuse in any form. We disguise anger because we feel it is socially unacceptable. Anger can be disguised behind the masks of silence, cynicism, or passive-aggressive behaviors like pouting, stubbornness, gossip, procrastination, and confrontation.

Don't repress your anger. Repression is the act of pushing angry feelings down to the unconscious mind so we don't have to deal with them. However, *anger* is emotional energy, and it manifests itself in disturbed thoughts, sleeplessness, constant irritability, passive aggression, angry outbursts, insomnia, tension in relationships, profanity, high-blood pressure, ulcers, and depression.

Don't explode with anger. Keep a lid on it. While it is healthy to express anger, it is unhealthy to express it by loud outbursts of rage. Choose a safe place and setting to properly express your feelings. When people rage, they get angrier, not less angry. We've seen peaceful protest turns into riots because anger spreads like a wildfire as a group of people get out of control. Rage and venting only make things worse and don't resolve any issues personally or socially. If your expression of anger doesn't promote reconciliation and peace, you're taking the wrong approach.

Power Prescription

Now that we know what doesn't work, let's learn what does work for anger management.

Sort it out. Understand why you are angry. There is a big difference between temporary anger and chronic anger. Confront your own negative feelings head-on and take a close look at the root cause. Seek counsel to help you explore and understand your anger. Self-understanding leads to self-control. Insight leads to change.

Count the cost. Unresolved anger is highly destructive. I once read that an angry confrontation can erase twenty acts of kindness in a relationship. Anger takes a toll on our health and our relationships. Studies show that even highly emotional couples can have long-lasting marriages if they don't blame or insult each other. Anger can get us fired from a job, destroy a friendship, or jeopardize a career. Before you blow your cool, count the cost.

Let it out. Let out your anger to God in prayer. Tell God how you really feel. He can take it. Then, talk it out with your spouse, a friend, or a counselor. Talking is therapeutic. You may need to tell the person with whom you're angry. Do it constructively. Don't blame them for your anger. Just tell them you want to get it off your chest so you can clear the air between you. Whatever you do, don't bottle-up anger. If you do, one of two things will happen—you will explode or you will implode.

Set limits. Control your words and your actions when angry. Pray this prayer often: "May these words of my mouth and this meditation of my heart be pleasing in your sight, Lord, my Rock and my Redeemer" (Psalm 19:14). The Book of Proverbs tells us, "When words are many, sin is not lacking; so he who controls his speech is wise" (see 10:19). "A gentle answer turns away wrath, but a harsh word stirs up anger" (15:1). A gentle answer given to an angry person will deescalate the situation and help you maintain control of your own feelings.

After Thomas Edison invented the telephone, he was the keynote speaker at a conference. As the host introduced him, he credited Edison with being the first person to invent a talking machine. Thomas Edison corrected the remark by saying, "I'm not the first person to invent a talking machine. God invented the first talking machine. I am the first person to invent a talking machine that can finally be turned off!"

Give it up. Surrender the right to resentment. Don't get even; get empowered! A woman was angry at her family for leaving her out of part of the family financial inheritance. She believed she didn't get her fair part of the estate. She told me passionately, "I have the right to be bitter toward my family."

"No, not if you're a Christian," I blurted out (almost wishing I hadn't said anything because she was so mad).

As God's children, we give up the right to stay angry. You can get angry, but don't stay angry. Don't let the sun set on your anger. Forgive others just as God forgives you, and you will live free. E. Stanley Jones said, "My heart is glad and too great to be the enemy of anyone."

8
SEX LIFE

"You shall not commit adultery."
EXODUS 20:14

A little girl brought home a document from school and was very upset. On the top of the card was her name, background information, and a box checked *F* for female.

"What's wrong, sweetheart?" her mother asked.

Pointing to the box marked *F,* she said with a shaky voice, "Look, Mom. I got an *F* in sex, and I haven't even learned about it yet."

When a married couple gets pregnant and announce it, everybody asks, "Is it a boy or a girl?" Our sexuality is set by our biology when we are conceived, and that is the basis of our identity. There are only two sexes—male and female. We develop a natural curiosity about sex when we are young.

A little boy and girl went to two different churches in a small rural town. He was Protestant and she was Catholic. They were playing by a creek and wanted to get in the water. They knew they would get in trouble if they came home with their clothes soaking wet. So, they decided to go skinny-dipping.

They took off their clothes and got ready to jump in. The little boy couldn't help but notice the obvious differences in their bodies. Staring at the little girl he said, "I never knew there was that much difference between Protestants and Catholics!"

Sexual love is a gift from God, but it comes with boundaries. Misusing the gift of sex has consequences. Sex education starts at home, not at school. Corrie Ten Boom tells of an experience with her father when she was young. They were traveling by train to their destination. When the train stopped and they were about to get off, she abruptly looked up at her father and said, "Daddy, what is sex?"

He was caught off guard by the question that came out of nowhere. He reached up to the luggage rack and got his suitcase. Putting it down on the floor, he said, "Corrie, would you please carry my suitcase for me?"

She took the handle and struggled trying to carry it.

"I can't pick it up, Daddy," she said, "it's too heavy for me."

Her father replied, "I know it's too heavy for you to carry. And what you've asked me to tell you about is too heavy for you to carry as well. You need to trust me to carry it for you until the right time when you are old enough and strong enough to carry it yourself."

Blessed Boundaries

In an age without sexual boundaries, we need the commandment of Exodus 20:14, "You shall not commit adultery." We need Biblical boundaries for sex. Boundaries are required for blessing. God says, "If you are willing and obedient you will enjoy the best of the land" (Isaiah 1:19). You will enjoy the best of life by living within God's boundaries.

Jesus explained the intent of this command. "You have heard that it was said, 'You shall not commit adultery.' But I tell you that anyone who looks at a woman lustfully has already committed adultery with her in his heart" (Matthew 5:27-28). Thoughts can turn into transgression.

Blessed boundaries means setting moral guidelines for your life. Morality comes from your personal ethics and values. The prophet Daniel "resolved not to defile himself" with the pagan culture of Babylon (Daniel 1:8). He made up his mind to live by godly convictions while living in a godless culture. Morality also comes from external sources such as social standards, family values, and religious teaching. What are your boundaries about sex? Are you following culture or Christ—society or Scripture?

Psychiatrist Karl Menninger, in *Whatever Became of Sin?*, stressed the importance of a moral code: "If the concept of personal responsibility for ourselves and for others were to return to common acceptance, and man would once again feel guilt for his sins and establish a conscience that would act for a deterrent for further sin, then hope would return to the world."[14] The word *sin* used in the Bible means "to miss the mark." Sin is falling short of God's standard of righteousness. Sin is disobeying God's Word. Sin is failing to live according to God's will and purpose for life.

---

[14] Karl Menninger, *Whatever Became of Sin?* (New York: Hawthorn Books, 1973).

The Bible also speaks of *fornication*, which describes various sexual sins, especially intercourse outside of marriage. "It is God's will that you should [live holy], that you should avoid sexual immorality; that each of you should learn to control your own body in a way that is holy and honorable, not in passionate lust like the pagans, who do not know God" (1 Thessalonians 4:3-5). Couples who are in love should avoid living together until they get married. Studies show that couples who live together are more likely to get divorced. Marriage is not something you "test drive." First, tie the knot and make the commitment; then you will discover the blessings of true sexual love in the covenant of marriage.

Sex is only for marriage. Biblical marriage only means a man and a woman in a covenant commitment. While the world may change the terminology of marriage, it can't change the truth of what God intended it to be. Jesus said, "But at the beginning of creation God made them male and female.' 'For this reason, a man will leave his father and mother and be united to his wife, and the two will become one flesh.' So, they are no longer two, but one flesh" (Mark 10:5-8). Jesus defined *gender sexual identity*, *marriage*, and *sex* all in that statement.

God blessed the sexual love shared between Adam and Eve at the dawn of creation. He told them, "Be fruitful and multiply." The Song of Solomon celebrates the beauty of erotic love between husband and wife in some of the most sensual language ever penned. Sex in marriage is for the pleasure of a couple to deepen their love and commitment to each other and for the sacred privilege of bearing children.

I saw a young man wearing a T-shirt in a shopping mall with the words: "Practice safe sex: Get married and be faithful!" Sex is only for marriage, and the Bible clarifies sexual sins and cautions us about the consequences of disobeying God. "Marriage is to be honored by all and the marriage bed kept pure, for God will judge the adulterer and all the sexually immoral" (Hebrews 13:4).

When it comes to sexual identity and sexual activity, God's people must not follow the world. The world is lost and in need of redemption. "Do not conform to the pattern of this world, but be transformed by the renewing of your mind" (Romans 12:2). The Scripture, not society, gives us sexual boundaries. True sex education comes from the Word, not from the world.

Adultery Analyzed

While *adultery* refers to unfaithfulness—specifically, extramarital affairs—this word is also used in Scripture to refer to sexual misconduct. Sexual sins are different from all other sins because they constitute a violation of one's own body and can cause emotional pain and physical illness (1 Corinthians 6:18). The Book of devotes two and a half chapters to the damage done by adultery. "But a man who commits adultery [lacks judgment]; whoever does so destroys himself" (Proverbs 6:32).

The wisdom of God cautions men:

Do not lust in your heart after her beauty or let her captivate you with her eyes. For a prostitute can be had for a loaf of bread, but [the adulteress] preys on your very life. Can a man scoop fire into his lap without his clothes being burned? Can a man walk on hot coals without his feet being scorched? So is he who sleeps with another man's wife; no one who touches her will go unpunished (Proverbs 6:25-29).

Adultery is also a form of covetousness and greed. "Do not covet your neighbor's wife," says the tenth commandment.

As a pastor and a licensed therapist, I've worked with married couples trying to cope with an affair. I can tell you that healing is possible! An affair does not have to be the end of a marriage. "Where sin increased, grace increased all the more" (Romans 5:20). If a couple is still in love, committed to surviving the devastating blow of an affair and seeks God for saving grace, they can put the pain behind them and move forward with a happy marriage. Jesus said, "With God all things are possible" (Matthew 19:26).

Why do people have affairs? Research shows the three primary causes of affairs are loneliness caused by emotional distance, monotony in the marriage and sex life, and poor communication about what they need and want from each other. *Time* magazine once featured a cover story about adultery titled, "Infidelity: It May Be in Our Genes." *Genetics* is sometimes a scientific term for our sin nature. When Jesus talked about adultery, he said, "Out of the heart of men, proceed evil thoughts, adulteries, fornications, murders" (Mark 7:21 NKJV). When we blame genetics, we're simply acknowledging original sin. Adultery comes from sinful desires, and it can only be conquered by the saving grace of God and the power of the Holy Spirit. "Walk by the Spirit, and you will not gratify the desires of the flesh" (Galatians 5:16).

An intimate marriage that is filled with love, affirmation, companionship, open communication, and sexual satisfaction is the key to affair-proof your marriage. "May your fountain be blessed, and may you rejoice in the wife of your youth. A loving doe, a graceful deer—may her breasts satisfy you always, and may you ever be intoxicated with her love" (Proverbs 5:18). When my son David Paul was in middle school, he and his friend saw this verse in the Bible. He told me, "Hey, Dad, look what we found in the Bible. How cool is that!"

I told him, "Keep reading the Bible and you will find a lot of cool things that will guide you to a great life." The first Bible verse I taught him is Proverbs 4:7: "The beginning of wisdom is this: Get wisdom. Though it cost all you have, get understanding." The Bible gives us the wisdom we need for a successful marriage and blessed boundaries for sex.

Dedicated, Not Distracted

The famous author Ralph Waldo Emerson said, "The ancestor of every action is a thought." Sex starts in the mind. We think before we act. Job said, "I made a covenant with my eyes not to look lustfully at a young woman" (Job 31:1). Jesus spoke of committing adultery in the heart before it becomes an action.

Marcus Aurelius, Roman philosopher, said, "Your life is what your thoughts make of it." Triumphant thinking equals transformed living! "Finally, brothers and sisters, whatever is true, whatever is noble, whatever is right, whatever is pure, whatever is lovely, whatever is admirable—if anything is excellent or praiseworthy—think about such things" (Philippians 4:8).

Married couples need to set boundaries. Avoid vulnerable situations. Jesus said, "The spirit is willing, but the flesh is weak" (Matthew 26:41). When Joseph was seduced by Potiphar's wife, he ran away from her. "She caught him by his cloak and said, 'Come to bed with me!' But he left his cloak in her hand and ran out of the house" (Genesis 39:12). Paul wrote, "Flee the evil desires of youth" (2 Timothy 2:22). If you follow the boundaries, you will enjoy the blessings!

Dedicate your body to God. "Do you not know that your bodies are the temples of the Holy Spirit? Therefore, honor God with your bodies" (1 Corinthians 6:19-20). The human body contains the soul and the spirit as you dedicate your whole self to God. Dedication equals deliverance. Your dedication to God will keep you from being distracted by temptation. "Therefore, I urge you, brothers and sisters, in view of God's mercy, to offer your bodies as a living sacrifice, holy and pleasing to God—this is your true and proper worship" (Romans 12:1).

Young people need to be taught to honor God with Biblical boundaries for sex. A close friend shared with me how he prepared his teenage son to face temptation. On his fifteenth birthday, he took his son to his favorite restaurant for dinner. After dinner, he handed his son a special gift. As the young man opened the present, he found inside a gold pendant with the cross of Christ.

My friend told his son, "You're growing up now. You will face temptations and will have to choose how you will live. This cross of Christ represents a covenant of purity with God. Wear it and ask Christ to protect you."

Just as Christ loved us and gave Himself for us, we must love Him and give up ourselves for His glory and honor.

9
ENTITLED TO EARN

"You shall not steal."

EXODUS 20:15

One of my greatest life experiences was getting my first job. I was sixteen and out of school for a summer of fun. My father changed my plan when he told me I was going to get a job for the summer.

He drove me to a new grocery store in our neighborhood, parked at the curb, and said, "Go introduce yourself to the manager and tell him you want a job." So, I went inside and talked to the manager about a job. He handed me an application, which I filled out and gave back to him. The manager placed my application at the bottom of a stack of other applications.

"When I have an opening, I'll give you a call," he assured me.

I left feeling pretty good. The stack of applications assured me of a great summer. He would never get to my application stuck at the bottom of the pile.

As I got back in the car, my dad asked me if I got a job. I said, "No, but I filled out an application," naively thinking this would appease my father. (I was about to learn the difference between a job and an application.)

My dad calmly said, "I didn't tell you to fill out an application but to get a job. Now go back in the store and tell the manager that you didn't come here to fill out an application, you came to get a job."

If you knew my dad, you would know I'm not exaggerating this story. I couldn't believe it. I was terrified to go back in there and face the manager, who didn't strike me as the most understanding man. But I mustered up the courage, went back in the store, and pleaded my case.

Knocking on the door again, he opened it quickly, took one look at me, and said rather sharply, "What do you want now?"

I said, "I just wanted to tell you that I didn't come in here to fill out an application. I came to get a job. I really need a job for the summer."

He was caught off guard by my assertiveness and looked at me in disbelief but said, "Okay. Let me see what I can do, and I will give you a call."

The next day was Saturday. The telephone rang at 8:00 in the morning. My mother called me to the phone. When I answered, it was the store manager telling me he had an opening for a job.

"When can you start working?" he asked.

Some people would want to chill out for the weekend and would've told the manager, "I'll be there Monday morning." (They're the ones who don't get the job.) I blurted out enthusiastically, "I'll be right there in a few minutes."

I ended up working at that store for my last three years of high school. They offered me management training in the company. I thanked them for the opportunity, but went on to college. That was the beginning of my work experience.

My father had given me the key to success—hard work! "All hard work brings a profit, but mere talk leads only to poverty" (Proverbs 14:23). I heard a pastor preach a sermon titled, "There Ain't No Shortcut to the Promised Land." How true!

Work Equals Wealth

While many people are being raised on entitlement, the only thing we are entitled to is to earn a living by hard work. We are entitled to earn, not to get something for nothing. Entitled people mistakenly think society owes them a living. They take but don't give. They consume but don't contribute. They make withdrawals on money they didn't deposit. They reap what they didn't sow. The best welfare is workfare. The best security is success.

God's commandment, "You shall not steal," teaches us work equals wealth. This commandment has a negative and a positive side. *Stop taking and start making!* You can have anything you want if you're willing to work for it. Everyone has the right and responsibility to work. In 1840, the French writer Alexis de Tocqueville observed about Americans, "To work is the necessary, natural, and honest condition of all men." Sadly, many people have lost the work ethic and are falling further behind financially. Politicians falsely promise citizens a free ride at the expense of others, while income inequality grows in America. People are saving less, living on credit, and looking to the government for provision.

A survey asked high school students in the United States and Japan to rate factors of success. Seventy-two percent of the Japanese students rated "hard work" first, compared to only 27 percent of the American students.

Some years ago, *The Futurist* magazine listed a "decline in work ethic" as a future trend affecting Americans. Today it's no longer a future trend but a present reality. Hard work, however, gives our lives meaning when we do our job well and contribute to our family, church, and community. While we must care for the poor and provide for those who cannot provide for themselves, it is the duty of every person to work. The Christian ethic states clearly, "If anyone will not work, neither shall he eat" (2 Thessalonians 3:10 NKJV).

I boldly told my father when I was eighteen, "I'm now an adult. I can do what I want."

He replied in a nice but firm way, "You're an adult when you move out of the house and pay all your own bills."

"Yes, sir." (I knew the other commandment about honor your father!)

A father and his teenage son clashed over an issue. The son had long shaggy hair, no job, and asked to use the car. His father refused until he cut his hair and got a job. The son objected, "But Jesus had long hair, and I want to be like Jesus."

The father said, "Fine. If you want to be like Jesus, you don't need the car. You can walk everywhere you go, just like Jesus did."

Inspiration or Perspiration?

Sir William Osler said, "The best preparation for tomorrow is to do today's work superbly well." It's an interesting phenomenon, but when we work harder, we get luckier!

When I was a senior in high school, I wrote a paper for English class on the life and work of American novelist William Faulkner. When asked what part inspiration played in his success, he said, "My work is 2 percent inspiration and 98 percent perspiration."

God created us to work. "The Lord God took the man and put him in the Garden of Eden to work it and take care of it" (Genesis 2:15). Here's the best kept secret of success—work it and take care of it! God placed us in the world to produce—so let's stop taking and start making. "Whatever your hand finds to do, do it with all your might" (Ecclesiastes 9:10). Your life is in your hands, so work with your hands with all your might and you will succeed. Your destiny is in your hands. If you are going to make it in life, you will have to work for it. "Whatever you do, work at it with all your heart, as working for the Lord, not for [men]" (Colossians 3:23).

Set the standard for excellence where you work. Get there early, dress well, stay off your cell phone, look for things to be done without having to be asked or told, take initiative, ask your supervisor for extra work, be grateful for your job, and tell those over you how much you appreciate the opportunity. Never cut corners, don't complain (a sure way to not get promoted) and let the way you work be a witness of your Christian values. "Make it your ambition to lead a quiet life: You should mind your own business and work with your hands, just as we told you, so that your daily life may win the respect of outsiders and so that you will not be dependent on anybody" (1 Thessalonians 4:11-12).

Sharing, Not Socialism

The dangerous doctrine of socialism has raised its head in America. Socialism is the enemy of success, independence, and wealth. *Socialism*, as defined by Karl Marx in *The Communist Manifesto*, is "the transition between capitalism and communism." A free-market economy celebrates and rewards individual work. People are free to determine their financial destiny. Socialism devalues the individual and only values the state. Karl Marx was an atheist and said religion is the opiate of the people—something to make them feel better so they can cope with life. The communist society is one devoid of God where people look to the state as God to provide for them.

Socialism has destroyed nations as people have served the state rather than striving for individual achievement. Marx's tenet of redistribution of wealth can easily become a form of stealing personal wealth and savings people have honestly and fairly earned from hard work. Governments are not entitled to people's personal property. Our is a government of the people, by the people, and for the people. In America, the government exists "for the people," not vice versa.

The early Christian church never practiced socialism, as some have suggested. Nothing could be further from the truth. Such ideology reinterprets Jesus through the lens of Karl Marx. Some people misinterpret the Pentecost experience of the church: "The entire group of those who believed . . . held everything in common. . . . then distributed to each person as they had need" (Acts 4:32, 35 CSB). Grace produces generosity.

The church freely shared what they had with each other during the festival. There is a big difference between freely sharing and forced socialism. Jewish people came from many nations to Jerusalem for Passover and Pentecost. Thousands of worshipers became Christians during these few weeks in Jerusalem. During their extended stay, they shared possessions with each other who needed assistance. After Pentecost ended, they returned to their respective towns and countries, where they lived and worked and took the gospel of Christ with them.

Socialism is dictated by the government, but the believers shared what they had with those in need. Furthermore, the gifts were only for people in the newborn church, not for everyone. They gave freely to God's people in the Christian community. Socialism is forced, not free will. Christians choose to give based on their individual decision, not because of government control. Christian giving is voluntary, based on love; not mandatory based on law. Sharing our wealth is a personal choice and what the Bible calls a free-will offering. "Each one must give as he has decided in his heart, not reluctantly or under compulsion, for God loves a cheerful giver" (2 Corinthians 9:6 ESV). You are free to give what you decide to give. It's called sharing, not socialism.

The Bible never advocates socialism as the economic theories of the day promote. Marxism is also based on agnosticism. In the case of the former Soviet Union and the current Chinese communist government, it's based on atheism, which explains why the individual is devaluated. Christians, however, believe every person is created by God and is self-determining. You are the master of your destiny, not the state. God has endowed us with free will. God designed us to live by choice, not by control. When Christians shared their resources with each other during Pentecost, it was voluntary and temporary to help those who had traveled long distances to Jerusalem from other nations. Later, they all went home to their countries and carried the Gospel with them.

Every person must work and earn their own money. Productivity is the only real solution to poverty and the secret to prosperity. We are also taught to generously share with other believers and to "remember the poor" (Galatians 2:10). The Christian church is deeply committed to caring for the poor, and we champion the cause of liberty and justice for all.

Liberation theology reinterprets Jesus through the lens of Marxism. Marx taught that religion was the opiate of the people to satisfy them until they learned to look to the state instead of to God. Socialism is an economic system where the government owns all property, and the individual owns nothing. The first tenet of socialism and communism is the abolition of all private ownership of property. The early church did not practice socialism. Community concern is not communist control. The New Testament rule for believers is, "Anyone who does not provide for their relatives, and especially for their own household, has denied the faith and is worse than an unbeliever" (1 Timothy 5:8).

The apostle Paul wrote:

> When we were with you, this is what we commanded you: "If anyone isn't willing to work, he should not eat." For we hear that there are some among you who are idle. They are not busy but busybodies. Now we command and exhort such people by the Lord Jesus Christ to work quietly and provide for themselves (2 Thessalonians 3:10-12 CSB).

The proper redistribution of wealth occurs with free trade, reasonable taxes based on representation, and generous free-will sharing with those in need. The greatest equality and equity are when everyone works for their own wealth so we are not dependent on anyone for anything. The Roman government was totalitarian like the communist party and oppressed its citizens, as well as the church. The government seized the property and assets of some Christians:

> Remember those earlier days after you had received the light, when you endured in a great conflict full of suffering. . . . You suffered along with those in prison and joyfully accepted the confiscation of your property, because you knew that you yourselves had better and lasting possessions (Hebrews 10:32, 34).

Government redistribution of wealth rarely gets money to the people in need. Years and years of government-sponsored social programs still leaves many of our inner cities and communities in poverty marked by failing schools, inadequate job opportunities, poor nutrition, and insufficient health care. The wealth seized goes to politicians and programs, but rarely to the people who need it the most. Socialism is not the same as social concern, social welfare, or social justice. Instead, it means one thing: The government owns everything, and the individual exists to serve the state. That's not Christian, and it never leads to a healthy economy. The Christian gospel is one of liberty. "Where the Spirit of the Lord is, there is freedom" (2 Corinthians 3:17). Any economic system that doesn't promote personal freedom to work, produce, build wealth, and promote generosity can hardly be called Christian.

We have a new term in America—*universal basic income.* What people need to succeed is *universal basic initiative.* We need to take the initiative to get ahead in life. We must give God something to bless. If we give God our best effort, He will bless us. God told Joshua and the people of Israel, "I will give you every place where you set your foot, as I promised Moses" (Joshua 1:3). There are two sides of this coin—the promise and the condition. God's promises come with conditions. The people of Israel had wandered in the desert for nearly forty years after missing their first chance to take the Promised Land. The promise must be possessed. When we work hard, we take the step to possess the promise of a successful life.

God will give you only the ground you are willing to take. Think of the phrase "set your foot." You walk and run with your feet. You pursue with your feet. Your feet symbolize movement and action. Use your feet to step, not to stand around and think somebody else is going to do it for you. My dad never let me stand doing nothing. He would tell me, "Son, get your hands out of your pockets." He wanted me to be ready.

Israel had to set their feet on new territory instead of going back to walking in circles in the desert. If you don't act and work hard, you will stay stuck where you are. You can claim your promised land when you set your foot on new territory. Get walking and working today, and you will succeed. You must work your way to wealth and, as you do, help others succeed too.

Money Views

One of Jesus' most famous stories is the parable of the Good Samaritan.

"One day a man was traveling the Jericho Road from Jericho to Jerusalem. Some thieves attacked him, stole everything he had and left him for dead. A priest passed by, noticed the man lying helpless by the road but went on his way. Later that day, a Levite, an assistant to the priests, also passed by but ignored the injured man.

"Then came the Samaritan. Moved with compassion, he helped the man. He bandaged his wounds and took him to the nearest inn. The Samaritan paid the innkeeper and instructed him to take care of the man until he could come back to check on him" (see Luke 10:30-35).

Charles Allen said this story shows three different views people hold about money.

What belongs to others is mine, and I will take it. The thieves who robbed the man believed the money he possessed belonged to them, so they stole it. He would have been safe if the thieves had obeyed God's commandment, "You shall not steal" (Exodus 20:15). Stealing is taking someone else's property. Entitlement promotes theft. People steal from others because they think they are entitled to it.

Theft has skyrocketed with cyber theft, home break-ins, and personal robberies. No one would think of owning a home or operating a business or securing a credit card without theft insurance. There were 4.8 million fraud and identity theft reports to the Federal Trade Commission in 2020, up 45 percent from the prior year. Consumers reported losing more than $3.3 billion related to fraud complaints—an increase of $1.5 billion from 2019. Our nation's capital, the District of Columbia, has the highest robbery rate in the country and the highest violent crime rate. On average, there are 500,000 shoplifting incidents per day and $13 billion worth of goods stolen from stores every year in America, which equals $35 million dollars of stolen items per day.

When something is stolen, God requires that restitution be made. In other words, we need to pay back what was stolen. Whatever was stolen needs to be returned. When I was a little boy, I stole a pack of bubble gum from the grocery store. I didn't think of it as stealing. I just saw how delicious it looked in its slick wrapper, so I picked it up and put it in my pocket.

As my mother and I got in the car to leave, I unwrapped the gum and put a big, delicious piece in my mouth. The tone in my mom's voice caused me concerned when she asked, "Where did you get that gum?"

Fear swept over me, knowing I was caught. So, I said, "I found it."

She snapped back, "You didn't find it—you stole it!" Now I was worried.

She stopped the car, turned around, and headed back to the store. She took me to the manager, instructed me to give the gum to him, and confessed my theft. She didn't do it to humiliate me but to help me. I handed him the gum and told him I was sorry.

He thanked me and (feeling sorry for me) said, "You can keep the gum."

My mom said, "No, he can't." She paid him for the gum but didn't allow me to keep it. She didn't want me to taste the sweetness of my sin but the bitterness of my theft so I wouldn't keep stealing when I grew up. The people who steal today didn't have a great mom like I did to teach them God's commandment, *You shall not steal.* Or, if they did, they didn't take the Word of God to heart.

I learned two valuable truths that day. First, don't take anything that's not yours. Second, if you have stolen something, make restitution. That means to pay it back, if possible.

What's mine is mine, and I will keep it. Now, back to the story of the Good Samaritan. The priest and the Levite passed by the man who had been robbed without helping him. Their attitude was, "What's mine is mine, and I will keep it."

One day when Jesus was teaching a large crowd of people, a man demanded, "Teacher, tell my brother to divide the inheritance with me."

Jesus responded in an unusual way. "Man, who appointed me a judge or arbiter between you?"

Then, He cautioned, "Watch out! Be on your guard against all kinds of greed; life does not consist in an abundance of possessions" (Luke 12:15). Jesus told His disciples, "Sell your possessions and give to the poor for where your treasure is there is your heart also." You see, success is measured by what we give not by what we get.

Jesus taught, "It is more blessed to give than to receive" (Acts 20:35). You will experience incredible purpose and pleasure from giving offerings to support the ministry of the church and to help those who are in need. Don't cling tightly to your wealth. Be generous as God is generous to you. "God loves a cheerful giver" (2 Corinthians 9:7).

My kids used to get so excited when a TV commercial advertised something for free. "Look, Dad it's free!" I reminded them of what has been called the wisdom of the ages: "There ain't no free lunch. Someone had to pay for it."

After a major riot in a city where looters smashed windows, robbed stores, and damaged property totaling millions of dollars, I heard a few liberal politicians comment that the looters were justified in stealing private property because they are angry with the system. Besides, they noted, insurance will pay for it. Actually, the taxpayers, store owners, and customers will end up paying for all the damage. Such politicians should never hold public office.

God created us to be channels of His blessings, not storehouses. God's blessings follow generous giving. "Give, and it will be given to you. A good measure, pressed down, shaken together and running over, will be poured into your lap. For with the measure you use, it will be measured to you" (Luke 6:38).

Farmers in China discovered the spiritual principle of generosity. Years ago, when they began to plant and harvest potatoes, many of them decided to keep the biggest potatoes for themselves and re-plant the smaller potatoes. Year after year, their potatoes grew smaller until, finally, they were about the size of a marble. Nature had taught them a bitter lesson. Life gets smaller when we take the biggest and best for ourselves and fail to give back our best.

What's mine is God's, and I will share it. This was the Good Samaritan's view of money. So, he bandaged the man's wounds, checked him into an inn so he could heal in a safe place, paid all the expenses, and later went back to make sure the wounded man was OK.

We don't really own anything because, "The earth is the Lord's, and everything in it" (Psalm 24:1). The first principle of Christian money management is that God owns it all, and He gives us wealth to manage in a way that honors Him. We are stewards of God's resources rather than owners. "Command those who are rich in this present world not to be arrogant nor to put their hope in wealth, which is so uncertain, but to put their hope in God, who richly provides us with everything for our enjoyment" (1 Timothy 6:17). Every good and perfect gift comes from God above!

A great philosopher observed God could have created a plant that would grow a loaf of bread; instead, He created wheat so we could plant it, harvest it, and bake bread. God made us partners in creation. When you share what you have with others, you become God's partner in ministry. "We are God's fellow workers" (1 Corinthians 3:9 ESV). God is looking for workers. As Christians, we can focus so much on faith that we forget, "Faith [without works] is dead" (James 2:17). Wealth follows work 100 percent of the time. All successful people work hard to achieve their success.

After graduating from college, I headed out west to California. I served as an evangelist preaching at various churches every week. I lived for the first few months in Lakeside, outside of San Diego. I assisted the pastor and his wife, who were well up in years, with their small church. Pastor and Mrs. Thompson were like parents to me during the time I lived with them. The church facility consisted of a small sanctuary, fellowship hall, and two meeting rooms for classes on about two acres of land.

The Thompsons had given everything they owned for the Gospel. They lived in the back of the church, in one of the classrooms. They also had an RV that was parked next to the church, where I lived for the first couple of weeks. I was then given a sofa bed to sleep on in the fellowship hall. I only got to enjoy that bed for three nights. I arrived back at the church one afternoon to find that Mrs. Thompson had sold my bed in a rummage sale to make some money for the church. They gave me an army cot in its place.

I woke up every morning with a backache from sleeping on that cot with the sounds of the television blaring because she was hard of hearing. Also every morning, Mrs. Thompson cooked a homemade breakfast in the church kitchen with pancakes, bacon, eggs, and biscuits.

One day, Pastor Thompson and I were working on the church. I was thinking of all they had accomplished, and remarked to him, "You know, it's fantastic what God has done here at this church and the property."

He spun around and looked at me as though I had offended him. He said confidently, "Let me tell you something, young man. You should've seen this place when God had it all by Himself!"

Pastor Thompson was God's fellow worker. God did His part, and Pastor Thompson did his part. God is with you, but He won't do your work for you. You've got to give God something to bless. Just as God put Adam in the Garden of Eden to work it, He has placed you where you are to work and to produce for His glory, your gain, and the good of others.

God blesses our faith, our plans, and our effort. Faith is active, not passive. The Word of God admonishes us:

"Anyone who has been stealing must steal no longer, but must work, doing something useful with their own hands, that they may have something to share with those in need" (Ephesians 4:28).

The commandment to not steal is a negative way of saying, get to work! In a day of entitlement, we need to remember that success depends on working for what we want. "All hard work brings a profit" (Proverbs 4:23). If we work, we will prosper and have something to share with others. The Good Samaritan teaches us the proper view of wealth: *What's mine is God's, and I will share it.*

10
TELL THE TRUTH

"You shall not give false testimony."
Exodus 20:16

In the early days of jet aviation, Boeing and Douglas Aircraft were competing fiercely for sales to Eastern Airlines, which was headed by Eddie Rickenbacker. He told Donald Douglas that their specifications for the DC-8 plane were close to Boeing's in everything but noise suppression. Then he gave Douglas one last chance to make a better offer than the competition. After consulting with his engineers, Donald Douglas reluctantly told Rickenbacker he couldn't do it.

Rickenbacker replied, "I know you can't. I just wanted to see if you would be honest about it. You just secured an order for $135 million. Now go home and silence those jets!"

Let me ask you—is honesty always the best policy? I watched a television program about honesty. Three people were asked, "If $1,000 suddenly appeared in your bank account and you knew it was because of an error in banking accounting, would you report it to the bank?" Everyone said no, and they all gave reasons to justify their dishonesty. One woman said she would use the money now but pay it back later!

A radio talk show opened their program by saying, "Now something you can finally use from Washington: the truth, the whole truth, and nothing but the truth." Citizens would certainly love to hear the truth, the whole truth, and nothing but the truth from Washington, D.C. The political rhetoric of the day is so laden with half-truths, empty promises and even outright lies, that people are disillusioned with politics.

I saw a bumper sticker on a car that read, "Don't Vote; It Only Encourages Them!"

What Is Truth?

The Old Testament prophets called for truth in their day. "Truth has stumbled in the streets, honesty cannot enter. Truth is nowhere to be found" (Isaiah 59:14-15). Jeremiah said, "Truth has perished; it has vanished from their lips" (Jeremiah 7:28). The prophet Daniel described the immoral climate of the day by saying "truth was thrown to the ground" (Daniel 8:12). Zechariah looked for the day that "Jerusalem will be called the City of Truth" (Zechariah 8:3 NKJV). Our nation's capital can genuinely serve the people when it, too, is a city of truth.

Pilate asked Jesus, "What is truth?" Every person needs to answer the question to really live their best life. Jesus answers the question by saying, "I am the way and the truth and the life" (John 14:6). If you measure everything by the standard of Christ, you will live free! Jesus is the touchstone of truth. If what you hear, read, or think doesn't measure up to what Jesus taught; it's simply not true.

The Apostle John wrote: "I have no greater joy than to hear that my children are walking in the truth" (3 John 4). As a father, I feel the same way about my kids. As I pastor, I feel the same way about my people. As a counselor, I feel the same way about my clients. Honesty is the best policy. Honesty creates good health. Truth is the greatest virtue. Without truth, life is a sham. Truth creates trust, which is the foundation of healthy relationships. We trust God because He is true and faithful. We trust people who are genuine and real. Trust naturally follows truth.

Some people tell the truth only if it benefits them. A woman needed to get an airline ticket while at the airport. Her son was about eight years old, but he was small for his age. Since kids age five and under flew for half price, she told him that if anyone asked how old he was to say that he was five.

As the ticket agent processed her ticket, she asked the little boy, "How old are you?"

"I'm five," he answered.

She replied, "Do you know happens to little boys who lie about their age?"

He said, "Yes ma'am. They get to fly for half price!"

Honest to God

The ninth commandment, *You shall not bear false witness against your neighbor,* is a call for truth. God doesn't want religious rituals from us. He wants a personal relationship with us that's based on truth. People who play religious games with God and hide behind their façade forget He knows everything about them. Hiding from God is like kids playing hide-and-seek who think no one can see them if they just close their eyes.

Jesus confronted religious pretense in his day: "Woe to you, teachers of the law and Pharisees, you hypocrites! You clean the outside of the cup and dish, but inside they are full of greed and self-indulgence. . . . You are like whitewashed tombs, which look beautiful on the outside but on the inside are full of the bones of the dead and everything unclean" (Matthew 23:25-27).

The word *hypocrite* comes from a Greek word meaning "an actor on a stage." A hypocrite plays a part to deceive to take advantage of people. Hypocrisy doesn't mean imperfection. Nobody's perfect. Jesus was confronting the intentional duplicity between public image and personal integrity. We all need to close the gap between our private life and public image and, thereby, achieve wholeness. Healthy people are whole while unhealthy people are fragmented.

We can't hide because God knows everything. When Adam and Eve sinned, they hid from God because they were ashamed of their disobedience. They were afraid God would find out what they did. God came looking for them in the garden. He called for them, "Adam, where are you?" He didn't ask the question because He couldn't find Adam. God was asking, "Adam, where are you in your relationship to me?"

Forgiveness requires us to come out of hiding and be honest about our sins, mistakes, and wrongdoings. Forgiveness follows confession. "If we confess our sins, he is faithful and just and will forgive us our sins and purify us from all unrighteousness" (1 John 1:9). Let's stop hiding so we can be healed in the presence of a loving God.

I learned to tell the truth early in life. I watched my older brother get into trouble for lying when my parents confronted him. When he disobeyed my parents, he wouldn't admit it until they finally got him to confess. At least that's what my mother told me about him. She told me when I was an adult how my brothers and sisters were all different. She said, "David, you were an open book." I just admitted what I did, took the punishment and got it over with so I could go play. That's how we need to be with God. We need to be candid with God and bring everything out in the open when we pray so we can deal with the real issues in our hearts.

It's Not My Fault!

We don't like to confess our mistakes and wrongs. We prefer to blame somebody else. Blame shifting is one of the reasons many people don't grow up. Personal responsibility is the foundation of maturity and success. Psychiatrist William Glasser, in his book *Reality Therapy*, says, "People do not act irresponsibly because they are ill; they are ill because they act irresponsibly."[15] The victim cries, "It's not my fault!" The victim blames other people and circumstances for their problems. We have no-fault auto insurance, no-fault divorces, and no-fault morality.

Victimization now borders on the absurd. A Boston court acquitted Michael Tindall of flying illegal drugs into the country. His attorney argued that he was a victim of "action addict syndrome," a disorder that makes a person crave dangerous, thrilling situations. They said Tindall was not a drug dealer, only a thrill-seeker.

An Oregon man who tried to kill his ex-wife was acquitted on the grounds that he suffered from "depression-suicide-syndrome," whose victims deliberately

---

[15] William Glasser, *Reality Therapy: A New Approach to Psychiatry* (New York: Harper & Row, 1965), xvi.

commit poorly planned crimes with the unconscious desire of being caught or killed. His attorney argued that he didn't really want to shoot his wife, he wanted the police to shoot him.

The famous "twinkie syndrome" case of Dan White, who murdered San Francisco mayor George Moscone, is most bizarre. His attorney blamed the crime on Dan's emotional distress linked to his junk-food binges. Acquitted of murder, he was convicted on a lesser charge of manslaughter.

In Maryland a bodybuilder broke into six homes, set fire to three of them and stole cash and jewelry. A judge ruled him not criminally responsible because his use of steroids left him suffering from organic personality syndrome. The punishment? No jail time. Pop psychology has conjured up so many new addictions that no one takes responsibility and society doesn't hold people responsible.

Blame Game

People blame the devil, society, genetics, government, environment, education, media and on and on. A new wave of biological determinism let's people off the hook, giving them unjustified justification for their bad behavior and poor choices. Gene-mapping gives people the excuse of genetic determinants of behavior to justify the belief that all acts of misconduct is someone's fault. You're not responsible for what happens to you, but you are responsible for what you do about it. You can play the victim and indulge in self-pity, or you can live as a victor and rise with eagle's wings and soar to a great life!

Elaborate excuse systems are used to keep us from being honest about our misbehavior. The most common excuse is, *I didn't do it.* The excuse comes as a denial, an alibi, or an accusation of someone else. It's the story of Adam and Eve. When God confronted Adam with his sin, he said, "The woman you gave me, gave me the fruit to eat." He blamed God and Eve in one excuse—"The woman You gave me." When God confronted Eve about her disobedience she said, "The serpent deceived me." The serpent represents the devil's deception. At least she didn't blame God. People still like to blame the devil. But God's question to them was "what have YOU done?"

When Moses was on the mountain receiving the Ten Commandments for forty days, the people got tired of waiting on him and thought he wasn't coming back. They told his brother Aaron to make them a golden calf to worship. The golden calf was a Canaanite god, so they were already adopting the idolatry of the new land where they were destined. Aaron was the first high priest; however, he granted their request. What a poor example of a spiritual leader! A minister should serve God's will, not the whims of the crowd. So, Aaron collected all their jewelry and made the golden calf. The people started dancing wildly in honor of the idol without any restraint.

About that time, Moses came down from Mount Sinai holding tablets inscribed with the Ten Commandments. He just left the awesome presence of God only to find God's holy people worshiping an idol. To make matters worse, his big brother led the way by making the golden calf. When Moses demanded Aaron to explain his actions, he gave the most outrageous excuse. "I told them, 'Whoever has any gold jewelry, take it off.' Then they gave me the gold, and I threw it into the fire, and out came this calf!" (Exodus 32:24).

The second common excuse is, *It wasn't that bad.* People minimize their misbehavior. We justify our wrongdoing by providing a list of good reasons, or we minimize the damage done by our wrongdoing. The Bible tells us, however, that "all wrongdoing is sin" (1 John 5:17).

The third common excuse is *Yes, but. . . .* We start to admit our guilt only to reverse the confession by giving a good reason. I couldn't help it. I didn't really mean it. It's because I had painful past. I was in a bad mood. It's just my personality. This last excuse enables us to separate who we are from what we do so that we don't have to assume responsibility.

God asks you and me, what have *you* done? God doesn't ask what did someone else do? He asks what did you do? That's the question that holds each person accountable for his or her actions. Only you can hold yourself accountable to God, to others and to your conscience. Playing the victim leads to self-pity, personal irresponsibility, and spiritual immaturity. Taking responsibility leads to a life of empowerment, success, and influence. God expects honesty. He has no greater joy than for His children to walk in truth. When you do wrong, confess your sins to God, receive forgiveness, and learn from your mistakes. Healthy people are honest people.

Real Relationships

God's Word tells us plainly, "Speak the truth to each other, and render true and sound judgment in your courts" (Zechariah 8:16). Telling our innermost secrets and personal struggles to another person is risky. Transparency is predicated on trust. Don't share your struggles and sins without someone you can't trust unless you want to see your personal business posted on social media. How do you know if you can really trust someone? If you must ask someone, "Can I trust you?", then you can't! You know in your heart who you can really trust.

I'll never forget getting a D on my report card in ninth-grade algebra. My mother was strict about making good grades. However, algebra and I didn't get along well. Rather than face her, I foolishly decided to change the D to a B with a simple stroke of a pin. Before I got home, I felt guilty. Dishonesty is difficult for me. So, I tried to change the grade back from a B to a D.

The problem is D can be changed to look like a B but not vice versa. I ended up with an ink blob on the report card. Now I was super anxious about facing my mom. She was going to be disappointed by the grade (even though I worked hard for that D) and very angry by the attempted ruse. The first thing I did when I got home was to give the report card to my mother. I confessed what I did wrong and how I tried to undo it. She didn't believe my confession, so I was on lockdown studying algebra every night for a while. Believe me, I caused myself a lot of unnecessary grief.

Confession plays an important role in healing. "Confess your sins to each other and pray for each other so that you may be healed" (James 5:16). You don't need to broadcast all your faults to everyone but share them with a friend, parent, or minister you can trust. James goes on to say, "The prayer of righteous person is powerful and effective." The most important confession, and usually the only one needed, is made privately in prayer where God forgives our sins and heals our hearts.

I received a letter of confession from a gentleman. He poured out his heart as he confessed his sins. Later, he apologized for dumping all that stuff on me. I told him that his secret was safe with me and I was proud of him for writing it. His letter took a lot of courage. He felt a lot better for sharing his feelings with someone who cared about him, who wouldn't judge him and who would pray for him. In psychology, we call that a *catharsis in psychology*, which is a cleansing of psychic distress and toxic emotions.

Early in my ministry, a young man came to see me for counseling. He had been married for about a year. He poured out his heart and said, "Pastor, I've done something terrible." He went on to say, "Last week I yielded to temptation, and I had a one-night affair." He told me he had no interest in the woman, how much he loved his wife, and that he was shocked and ashamed by what he had done.

"I've confessed my sin to God," he told me, "But I don't know if I should tell my wife." He asked me what he should do. "Should I tell my wife? If I confess, she may not understand and may leave me. If I don't tell her, then I don't know if I can live with the guilt." As a counselor, I don't tell people what to do. Each person must make their own choices because they're responsible for the results. However, the Word of God gives us the answer. "Confess your sins to each other so that you may be healed." Hiding is never God's way. Healing follows honesty.

During a marriage counseling session, a woman stopped in the middle of what she was saying and blurted out, "I just realized how I have deceived myself." Whether we want to admit it or not, we can deceive ourselves. It's easy to tell yourself what you want to hear. We like to get others to confirm our viewpoints rather than have people challenge them. Only God can reveal what is really in our hearts. Let's pray, "Search me, O God, and know my heart; test me and know my anxious thoughts. See if there is any offensive way in me, and lead me in the way everlasting" (Psalm 139:23-24).

Hurdles to Honesty

Honest living requires us to jump three hurdle—rationalization, justification, and projection. *Rationalization* means believing our sins aren't as bad as the sins of others. We compare ourselves to worse sinners. "I'm not as bad as other people," we tell ourselves. However, that's the wrong comparison. We need to compare ourselves to the standard of Christ's perfection and to the will of God. When we do, we admit "all have sinned and fall short of the glory of God" (Romans 3:23).

Justification is telling ourselves we're an exception to the rule. In his classic novel, *War and Peace,* Leo Tolstoy's primary character Pierre is convicted of his sins but makes the mistake of praying, "O Lord, I have sinned, but I have several excellent excuses."

Frederick the Great once toured a prison in Berlin. As he walked along the rows of cells, the prisoners fell to their knees beseeching him to free them. They all proclaimed their innocence, except for one man who remained silent. Frederick had the silent man brought to him.

He asked, "Why are you here?"

The man answered, "Robbery."

Frederick asked, "Are you guilty?"

The man answered truthfully, "Yes, sir, I am. I'm guilty as charged."

Frederick ordered the man to be released immediately with a full pardon. The man thanked him and asked why. He replied, "You are a guilty man. I will not have you in this prison corrupting these fine, innocent people who occupy it."

Projection is focusing on the sins of others, so we don't have to focus on our own sins. We project our faults on others and judge them for doing the things we do. After all, it's easier to see other people's sins than it is our own. It's certainly easier to judge others than judge ourselves. The Apostle Paul wrote, "Examine yourselves . . . test yourselves" (2 Corinthians 13:5). Plato said, "The unexamined life is not worth living."

We often feel that God won't forgive us. One man said to me, "I feel worthless." God loves us just like we are and understands who we are and why we do what we do. So, be honest with God and you'll find healing in His presence.

A Scottish theologian named John Duncan of New College in Edinburgh went to a church on Sunday. When holy communion was served, he saw a young woman refuse to take the sacrament. He discerned by her body language that she felt unworthy to take the bread and the wine. So, he whispered to her, "Take it. It's for sinners."

One of my favorite sayings of Jesus is, "It is not the healthy who need a doctor, but the sick. I have not come to call the righteous, but sinners to repentance" (Luke 5:31-32).

To Thine Own Self Be True

While attending college, as a psychology major, I read a little book titled, *Why Am I Afraid to Tell You Who I Am?* It changed my life. The spiritual and psychological truths the author presents set me free to be myself without fear of rejection or not measuring up. You see, I told myself that I must be perfect to be worthwhile. That is the life script of a perfectionist. Such irrational beliefs set a person up for feeling inadequate because nobody is perfect. The perfectionist always falls short of their belief that they must be perfect.

Instead of expressing myself, I would try to appease what I thought people wanted from me and conform to peer pressure. I didn't realize that God, my parents, and my friends loved me for who I really am and that I don't need to play the part for people to love and appreciate me. When you are true to yourself without fear of rejection, then you are truly free to live.

When people put pressure on you to meet their expectations, you lose yourself. If we aren't true to ourselves, we become a reflection of people's expectations. I once heard my pastor say in a sermon, "Do God's will and do what you want to do, and don't worry about anything else." That statement inspired me to live my life for God's will and my aspirations. That's not selfishness, it's self-expression. It takes courage to be true to yourself without fear of rejection.

Young people compromise their convictions because they want to fit in with their peers. They fold under peer pressure because they want to be accepted. Young people need affirmation and affection. Peer pressure doesn't just happen to young people. Adults confront it too. A friend of mine shared an experience with me that happened to him on a business trip. He was out of town for a convention. After a long day of meetings, several of his partners planned to go out and party. They asked him to go, but he declined. They pressured him to go with them, but he stood his ground.

One guy asked, "Why don't you want to go and party? We're going to have fun."

He replied, "I'm a Christian and I'm married. I want to be true to my convictions and faithful to my wife." He told them to go ahead without him and have a good time.

A little while later, there was a knock at his hotel door. Opening the door, he saw two of the men from the group. They said, "We started to go but were convicted by your life and example. We're going to stay at the hotel as well." They all had a great dinner together at the hotel.

That man was true to himself. We don't have to preach to others or tell them how to live their lives. That's none of our business. Just be true to yourself and you impact others for Christ. Honesty, truthfulness, and genuineness is the best policy.

11
CONTENTED CONSUMERS

"You shall not covet."
Exodus 20:17

Paul Simon, in his song "American Tune," sings, "I don't have a friend who feels at ease." He put his finger on the feeling of discontentment. Do you feel at ease? Are you happy and satisfied? Contentment is an important part of being happy.

Marketers try to make us believe we will be happier if we get more stuff. It misleads us into thinking bigger is always better. It clutters our landscape with billboards. It floods our emails after every purchase we make with the message, "If you liked that, we think you will like this." If you watch a movie online, you get a message that says, "Watch more like that." It's always about getting more.

Our government is spending us into oblivion. Politicians don't seem to know the difference between printing money and actual money. My mother used to tell me, "David, money doesn't grow on trees." On average, Americans spend more than their annual income because of credit spending. Credit means spending money today that we hope to get tomorrow. Our national debt is growing at an alarming rate and deficit spending soars.

The word *content* means to be free from complaint and to be satisfied with what we have. When we are content, we can manage good times and bad times with the same level of happiness. Contentment from what we possess on the inside, not the outside. Contentment is a condition of our heart and mind that finds joy in what we have rather than being envious of what others have.

Contentment doesn't mean mediocrity, lack of drive, or laziness. While we set goals to achieve, we also need to enjoy life today as we press on for what lies ahead. My mother used to tell me, "David, slow down and smell the roses along the way." She said that because she likes gardening, but I got the point.

Contentment empowers us. "Better a little with the fear of the Lord than great wealth with turmoil" (Proverbs 15:16). Contentment is learned. Paul said, "I have learned to be content whatever the circumstances" (Philippians 4:11). He was in prison when he wrote those words. His contentment came from within.

We all like money, but we shouldn't love it. We should like things and love people. Contentment is important in our character development. "Godliness with contentment is great gain. For we brought nothing into the world, and we can take nothing out of it. But if we have food and clothing, we will be content with that" (1 Timothy 6:6-8). "Keep your lives free from the love of money and be content with what you have, because God has said, 'Never will I leave you; never will I forsake you'" (Hebrews 13:5).

No season of the year tests our contentment as much as Christmas does. We shop for gifts no one needs with money we don't have for people we don't like! One Christmas Eve a man went shopping at the mall to look for some last-minute gifts. He saw a very strange-looking devise on the counter. He couldn't figure out what it was, so he asked the salesperson, "What does it do?"

She replied, "It doesn't do anything. It's a Christmas gift."

Wealth Management

Our worth is not measured by our wealth. Money is integrally involved in every area of life. Ecclesiastes 10:19 says, "Money is the answer for everything." Now, that's an intriguing statement to find in the Bible. While building our wealth for our family is good stewardship, our worth as a person is greater than our wealth. Some people derive their self-esteem from their financial success, but our true worth comes from who we are as person created in God's image.

Money management begins with putting God first. "Honor the Lord with your wealth, with the first fruit of all your crops" (Proverbs 3:9). Moses reminds us, "Remember the Lord your God, for it is he who gives you the ability to produce wealth" (Deuteronomy 8:18). When we honor God with generous giving, we truly seek first the kingdom of God and make an impact in the world for His glory.

Money is a great employee but a terrible boss. "Whoever loves money never has enough; whoever loves wealth is never satisfied with their income" (Ecclesiastes 5:10). Don't let the pursuit or possession of money run your life. My father once turned down a job promotion for more money because it would've negatively impacted our family. He put his family above his finances. Let your values not your valuables be your top priority.

God promises to bless us financially when we manage our money according to His Word. "My God will meet all your needs according to the riches of his glory in Christ Jesus" (Philippians 4:19). Abraham called God *Jehovah-Jireh,* meaning "the Lord will provide." As King David reflected over his life, he penned the words, "I have never seen the righteous forsaken or their children begging for bread" (Psalm 37:25).

The love of money is not possessing money but rather money possessing you. God's great servants like Abraham did not let money possess them. Lydia was a wealthy businesswoman who supported Paul's ministry. When Jesus was born, magi came from the East and brought wealth in the form of gold, frankincense, and myrrh. Those gifts may have funded His public ministry. The work of the Gospel is supported heavily by those whom God has blessed with enormous wealth. God gives some people a supernatural anointing to make great wealth to fund the church and the gospel of Christ. The top one percent of wage earners pay most of the taxes in America that provide infrastructure, schools, military, social programs, and healthcare for everyone.

Anointed Advancement

Every person with drive and initiative wants to advance in their career and calling. God told Adam and Eve to be fruitful. He designed us to build and to plant and to aspire for great things in life. While you are advancing, enjoy where you are today. When Barbie and I got married, we lived in a duplex and enjoyed it as much as the house we own today. You don't have to wait to be happy; choose to be happy today. That's contentment.

You need to set goals to reach your potential. Contentment and ambition go together. Dream big dreams and pursue them passionately, but enjoy the here-and-now. Very successful people start at the bottom and work their way to the top. However, they enjoy every job along the way. So, if you get a job bagging groceries but you want to be the store manager, be the best employee you can be. When you become the manager or owner, you'll appreciate what you have.

One day while Francis of Assisi was working on his garden, a passerby asked him, "What would you do if you were suddenly to learn that you were to die at sunset today?"

He replied, "I would finish tending my garden."

Disarm Discontentment

Let's get back to the tenth commandment, *You shall not covet*. The word *covet* comes from a Greek word meaning "grasping for more." People bound by covetousness are discontent in life. Covetous people envy what other people possess and enjoy—their possessions, their position, and their prominence. They resent other people for their condition instead of improving their lifestyle.

Tim Kimmel defines *covetousness* as "material inebriation. It's an addiction to things that don't last and a craving for things that don't really matter." Discontentment complains, "If only."

If only I had a job, a better job, a more understanding boss, enough money to retire on, a bigger house, a thinner waist, a better education, a husband, a different husband, a child, a lifestyle like other people.

If only I had not dropped out of school, been forced to get married, had an abortion, started drinking, been fired, run up so many debts, neglected my wife, quit that job, sold that stock.

If only they had given me more playing time, recognized my potential, offered me the job, encouraged me in my sports, been honest with me, stuck with me.

If only they had not abandoned me as a baby, discouraged me, prejudged me, pushed me so hard to achieve, lied to me, been so interested in making money, been ashamed of my handicap.

If only . . . if only . . . if only.[16]

Be content with your person. Temptation to sin often starts with discontentment. You might take a negative view of your abilities, attributes, or appearance. You might wish you were someone else. I encourage you to celebrate who you are and aspire to be the best version of you that you can be.

Be content with your position. I played basketball in high school and in many competitive leagues. Teams have a few star players and a lot of role players. Five players start a basketball game, and the others come off the bench as called on by the coach. Even the starting five can be a different lineup based on the coach's game strategy. A good team consists of every player being content with their position on the team. Players don't go to the coach during a game and say, "Put me in the game, Coach." The coach will bury you on the bench if you do that. Good players are content with their position on the team, even though each player works hard to earn a higher position.

---

[15] Tim Kimmel, "Robbed of Rest," *Focus on the Family* (February 1988), 2-5.

Be content with your possessions. I've never met a person who didn't want to make more money. We naturally want to improve our standard of living. So, work hard, learn new skills, and make sound investments to grow your wealth, all the time being content, grateful, and happy. John the Baptist said, "Be content with your pay" (Luke 3:14).

A certain man tried to explain their financial problems to his wife. "Honey, there are the haves and the have-nots. The haves are the rich and the have-nots are the poor."

"What are we?" she asked.

He said, "We're the middle class. We are the haves who haven't paid for it yet."

Be content with your partner—your husband or wife. Extramarital affairs start with discontentment in marriage. God says, "You shall not covet your neighbor's wife." Married couples need to pursue each other passionately through every season of their life to protect their marriage against discontentment.

We don't need more things to be happy; we need to enjoy what we have. Charles Boswell was a football star at the University of Alabama. He was destined for a promising career in the NFL. However, he lost his eyesight in combat during World War II. He began playing golf during his rehabilitation, and went on win the National Blind Golf Championship seventeen times.

When an interviewer asked him how he overcame the loss of his sight and determined to be a professional golfer, he said, "I never count what I've lost. I only count what I have left." That statement is the best definition of contentment I've ever heard.

Freely Give

Desires need to be disciplined, not over-indulged. When Barbie and I got married, my mother gave us a book on managing money. (She knew I needed to read it!) The author said before a couple makes a major purchase they should ask if the item is a need, a want, or a desire. Asking that question helps develop contentment and avoid excessive consumerism.

We need to eliminate envy and cultivate contentment.

What causes fights and quarrels among you? Don't they come from your desires that battle within you? You desire but do not have, so you kill. You covet but you cannot get what you want, so you quarrel and fight. You do not have because you do not ask God. When you ask, you do not receive, because you ask with wrong motives, that you may spend what you get on your pleasures (James 4:1-3).

Generosity curbs covetousness. When we give our tithes and offerings to support the work Lord, we invariably don't spend all our money on ourselves. When we help those who are less fortunate, we get outside ourselves and live the extended life. Personality theorist Gordon Allport described the mature personality as a person whose highest quality is "the extension of the self." Make all you can make, save all you can save, and give all you can give. "Anyone who has been stealing must steal no longer, but must work, doing something useful with their own hands, that they may have something to share with those in need" (Ephesians 4:28). One of the reasons Christians work is so they will have something to give. We earn income not only for ourselves and our families but also to give to help others in need.

The birth of America occurred on July 4, 1776, with the signing of the Declaration of Independence. Before that time, the colonies were part of Great Britain. Early settlers and pilgrims came to America for many different reasons over many years. The American Dream began with a desire and a declaration to be free from government control and excessive taxation, according to history. Democracy thrives on personal freedom, free markets, and private ownership. Socialism and communism are systems of class warfare to the point that private property is seized by the government, which, in turn, owns and controls everything. Income redistribution can be theft by another name if the government takes too much from the people who earn it. Taxation must always be based on representation.

On the other hand, greed and corporate abuse of employees by paying unfair wages is also a great sin. "Greed ... is idolatry" (Colossians 3:5). The greatest idol is money. Everyone and every corporation should pay their fair share of taxes as we share in the common good of society. Sound economic policies must provide for the poor, prevent discrimination, and guarantee the rights of every worker to earn fair wages so people can build and keep their own wealth, as well as generously share their possessions freely and not by force. Jesus said, "Freely you have received; freely give" (Matthew 10:8).

God gives a strong word to business owners, corporations, and governments: "Woe to those who make unjust laws, to those who issue oppressive decrees, to deprive the poor of their rights and withhold justice from the oppressed of my people, making widows their prey and robbing the fatherless" (Isaiah 10:1-2).

Gratitude Attitude

Covetousness manifests itself by complaining about who we are, where we are, and what we have. One night Matthew Henry, a Bible scholar, was robbed. When he got home, he was shaken from the event but wrote a powerful prayer:

> Father, I thank You first because I was never robbed before. Second, I thank You because although they took my money, they did not take my life. Third, I thank You because although they took everything I had, it wasn't very much. Finally, I thank You because it was I who was robbed and not I who robbed.

Gratitude insulates us against covetousness. "Give thanks in all circumstances; for this is God's will for you in Christ Jesus" (1 Thessalonians 5:18).

After a Bible study at our church, I greeted a man and asked, "How are you doing?"

He replied, "I'm doing great now that I've been to the Bible study. I came here feeling disappointed because I didn't get the job promotion I expected. I've been angry with God and discouraged. I've been jealous of others. I've been complaining that life isn't fair. I got focused on what I didn't have. But today, I have regained my perspective. I have new joy. From now on, I am going to focus on my haves and not my have-nots!"

Here's a great parable about contentment I heard. Once upon a time, there was a man who lived with his wife, two small children, and his elderly parents in a tiny hut. He tried to be patient and gracious, but the noise and crowded conditions wore him down.

In desperation, he consulted the village sage about his unhappiness. "Do you have a rooster?" asked the wise man.

"Yes," he replied.

"Keep the rooster in the hut with your family and come see me again next week."

The next week the man returned and told the wise man that his living conditions were worse than ever, with the rooster crowing and making a mess of the hut.

"Do you have a cow?" asked the sage. The man nodded hesitantly in the affirmative. "Then, take your cow into the hut and come see me next week."

Over the next several weeks, the man was instructed to put his goat, two dogs, and his brother's children in the hut.

Finally, he couldn't take the crowded, chaotic living conditions anymore. So, he got rid of the animals and told everyone to leave except his wife, kids, and parents. The hut suddenly became spacious and quiet, and everyone was happier than ever.

Ordinary Joy

Contented people have discovered the joy of the ordinary life. Remember, covetousness means grasping for more. The constant comparison of what we have with others only leads to envy, jealously, vying for power, and a complaining spirit.

The desire for greatness has corrupted many good men and women. Seek goodness, not greatness, and you will discover true greatness. One of the quiet leaders behind the scenes in the early church was Barnabas. The Bible simply says of him, "He was a good man" (Acts 11:24). Would you rather be great or good? Do you prefer to be better or better off? The Grecian king Alexander was called "the Great" because he conquered the world, but he was never called "good." I talk to many pastors who are obsessed with being an influencer or leader, however, Jesus called us to be servants. "Whoever wants to become great among you must be your servant" (Matthew 20:26).

When we serve, we naturally exert a positive influence on others. Leadership isn't learned; it's lived. People know it when they see it, and they follow it naturally. Many people have the title, but they don't have the trait of a true leader—someone who finds joy in service rather than in success. As Christians, we are called to follow the example of Jesus, who wrapped a towel around his waist and washed the disciples' feet. That is leadership. When He finished washing their feet, He told them, "I have set you an example that you should do as I have done for you" (John 13:15).

When Harry Truman was thrust into the presidency by the death of President Roosevelt, a friend took him aside and gave him some great advice. He told him, "From now on, you're going to be surrounded by lots of people. They'll try to put up a wall around you and cut you off from any ideas but theirs. They'll tell you what a great man you are, Harry. But you and I both know you ain't."

The following insights were written by Dr. Bob Moorehead, longtime pastor of Seattle's Overlake Christian Church:

> The paradox of our time in history is that we have taller buildings, but shorter tempers; wider freeways, but narrower viewpoints; we spend more, but have less; we buy more, but enjoy it less. We have bigger houses and smaller families; more conveniences, but less time; we have more degrees, but less sense; more knowledge, but less judgment; more experts, but

more problems; more medicine, but less wellness. We have multiplied our possessions but reduced our values. We talk too much, love too seldom, and hate too often. We've learned how to make a living, but not a life; we've added years to life, not life to years.

We often pursue a false sense of greatness in terms of fame, fortune, power, and pleasure. Mother Theresa said, "Maybe you can't do great things for God. But you can do good things with a great heart." The extraordinary life is discovered in doing ordinary things.

Jean Paul Richter said, "Do not wait for extraordinary circumstances to do good; try to use ordinary situations." You don't have to be perfect, or better than everybody else, or always finish first to be successful. Just do *your* best. Avoid comparing yourself and your achievements with those of others. Be content with who you are and what you have. Then you'll discover the joy of the ordinary life. Dr. Martin Luther King said, "Everyone can be great because everyone can serve."

At a Crossroads

Our journey through the Ten Commandments is now complete. We stand at a crossroads. Which path will we take? Will we follow the new morality of the day that leaves God out of our lives? Will we change our moral code to fit the present circumstance?

Your best life is found on the ancient path of God's unchanging Word. "Stand at the crossroads and look; ask for the ancient paths, ask where the good way is, and walk in it, and you will find rest for your souls" (Jeremiah 6:16).

Trust God's law, which is forever written on our hearts.